SCOUTS DISHONOR

By Tommy Womeldorf

Why are you so enchanted by this world, when a mine of gold lies within you? – Rumi

PROLOGUE

Sunday morning. The girls shook me awake again and I rolled over with an exaggerated grumble. My youngest daughter, Lola, climbed up on the bed to get a few quick jumps in.

"Is it church day, Daddy?"

It was. I tried to compose my mind as she jumped rhythmically between Arlene and me. My wife's still-sleeping form caught my attention. There was no way she could sleep through this. I reached out and put my arms around Fiona, who stood beside the bed.

"Where are your sisters?" I asked.

"Julia's watching TV and Sophia's still sleeping."

"Well, you'd better come here then."

I hauled her up on the bed just as Arlene rolled over and tackled Lola. The girls fell into a heap of rumpled sheets as we wrestled them into a fit of giggles.

"Parents win again!" I said when we'd sufficiently unsettled the bed sheets.

Getting out of bed, the girls continued to try to hang on me as I struggled toward the bathroom. I savored these moments, when the noise of my family was enough to banish the other thoughts. It was in the quiet and alone times, when I considered how to tackle another day of sobriety; another day of church and of living that I'd so often struggled. That's what many people don't realize: that it's a conscious effort every day to compose and prepare myself to live outside of the shadow.

After breakfast, we loaded our four chattering daughters into the car. That's when the tension started to build. Walking into the church was always an exercise in composure. I felt like an actor on a stage, playing the part. I greeted everyone with a smile and carried on conversations before the service with compassion that was genuine, even though a charade was being carried out all around us. Whenever I started to think this way, I would find Arlene in the crowd. Whether she saw me or not, it was enough just to look at her. I felt myself being grounded, and I gained from her the courage to go on.

That day, however, I noticed my frustration growing as I sat through the service. Recently, I'd become increasingly disenchanted with the church and the messages they delivered each week. No, that's not true. I'd long been disenchanted, but I'd tried to adapt and fit into the mold. I wondered if it was in my nature to do this, again and again.

As I sat there, listening to a message of tolerance, I was reminded again of just how much the church actually tolerated. I remembered sitting before the Bishop as a thirteen year old boy, with my father beside me, in the room where my long mistrust began. I remembered a coldness and a disconnection from what I had long been taught the Church and the elders stood for. I saw myself enter the following years in a state of emotional torment. I knew that these thoughts were leading me down a path I did not want to follow, but the shadow was creeping and it was like an addiction; once it had its grips on me, it was next to impossible to free myself.

In the next moment, darkness closed in on me and I

was in Pink again. In the old apartment building on Wilcox, two doors up from Hollywood Boulevard, everything from the molding to the bars on the windows was pink. I'd just come off of a bad trip and I was living there with Rich, who was the best friend I could ever hope for. I'd known him since we were ten years old and I'd lived with him a few times in the years since I'd been out on my own. I was used to his insomnia and he was used to me passing out from an alcohol or heroin binge and burning holes in my clothes or the couches with my cigarette.

The manager of the apartment building, Francisco, suspected us of being gay lovers (along with our parents and a few others), but that was probably just because Rich was kind of glamorous. I was clearly on yet another downward spiral, but Rich helped keep me going from day to day. That is, until he made plans to visit his sister in London for several months. When he told me this, I already sensed the darkness that lay ahead. I'd been getting strung out a lot worse and I didn't know how I might function on my own. The summer of 1999 was coming to an end and the dread and loneliness encroached, even before he left.

When Rich was gone, I started making new friends at the needle exchange on Cahuenga. These associations brought me to a series of shooting galleries and piss-soaked squat spots. Still, I managed to keep the people I met there away from Pink. I always met my main dealer in the Sri Lankan restaurant next door to avoid letting him know where I lived.

Then, after Rich had been gone a month, I completely fell apart. I spent days and nights alone and strung out until at last I was completely out of money and totally alone. I tried to stay perpetually medicated to take away the pain of feeling anything at all. It had become an accessible solution when no other alternative had been available, and now it was a habitual way of life.

With no money, I was at a dead end. I was going through the worst kick I'd ever been on. I tried the usual detoxing tricks of pounding cottons, wringing them out, and shooting dingy water. Nothing helped. It was then that I noticed one of Rich's two pet snakes had died. A horrible smell permeated the apartment; that smell that any living thing seems to recognize instinctively as death. Or perhaps I just noticed it because I was on the verge of such an untimely end myself. I'd always been afraid of snakes, although when I was trying to detox this fear took on a paralyzing quality. I did not go near the converted bookshelf in Rich's room where the corpse lay.

Francisco stopped by often asking for rent, which I didn't have a dime of. He asked me about the smell that emanated from the apartment and I told him I thought something had died in a crawl space somewhere. But I could see the terrified look in his eyes. He thought I had killed my gay lover, who hadn't been seen in over a month.

Meanwhile, I felt like I was the one dying, in the midst of so much pain and loneliness. My world was a dark place, and consisted of no more than the view from my bedroom window of the Pacific Theater building next door. I knew then that if I had the strength to walk across the street, I would have taken the elevator to the top and jumped off. Thinking this, I began to have delusions of how I might kill myself, and imagined clawing through the wall to the next apartment in hopes of finding a gun to end the pain with. Never had I known such despair in my life.

After three of the longest days of detoxing I could recall, I managed to take a shower. I shivered and dry-heaved the whole time, but I knew I had to keep going. I had to get out. It felt like it took hours just to dress myself. Yet in those hours I had the presence of mind to know that I was not living but dying. I was, in the great scheme of things, standing on that precipice at the edge of the Pacific Theater building as surely as if I had bodily climbed there.

It was a hot December day in Hollywood and the new millennium was on the horizon. I pushed open the door of the apartment building feeling like my next move might be my last. My eyes were malnourished and could barely stay open under the blinding white light of the boulevard. Yet the day's heat on my skin could be felt in every particle of my being. I closed my eyes and drifted on the waves of warmth. I stood on the corner, blinking under the sun.

Arlene squeezed my hand and I could feel the gentle pressure of her body beside me on the pew. Lately I'd been restless. Church had become increasingly unsettling. I knew the reason for this of course. Arlene could sense when I was in a dark place, just as I could intuit when she was in hers. I became aware again of the lightness and glow of the church walls around me. Was I the only one to sense the heaviness in that room? I wondered often if I would ever be free of the burden. Or if the false brightness of that holy place would ever resolve to truthfulness and clarity. There had been times when the church meant something more to me, like when Arlene was first called to it and it meant a new life and new hope for our young family. There had been times when I despised it.

I excused myself near the end of the service and sat out the remainder on a bench in the hall. I knew my God and I knew the singular purpose He had given me. When my daughters came out after the service, they saw me and ran to sit beside me. Those were the moments that made it

5

worth it. Theirs was the innocence that meant the most to me.

I met Arlene's eyes and saw that she knew the significance of my struggle. That was the last time we went to church.

CHAPTER ONE

2012

Two weeks before, the August heat had been almost unbearable. It was the end of the summer of 2012 and I was reporting on Monday morning as an extra laborer on a job in Scottsdale, Arizona. My duties as an extra hand were to unload the back of the truck that carried the convention supplies. It was only when I pulled up behind the enormous truck at the rear of the hotel that I saw the words "Boy Scouts of America" printed on the side and realized who the job was for. Not surprisingly, the convention was held in the upscale, Mormon-founded Marriot hotel. The threads that connect the Mormon Church's web are often invisible, but can be seen almost anywhere if one looks close enough. Their connection with the Boy Scouts organization happens to be the one that snared me, but there are many more.

Twenty-nine years after the fact, and finding myself working for their convention didn't disturb me so much as fill me with a sense of irony. I greeted my buddy Will and we set to work rolling up the door of the trailer. Inside was a jumbled mess of equipment.

Will whistled. "Looks like this one might take a

while," he said while I grabbed the dolly and he unhooked the loading ramp from the bed of the truck.

We were used to seeing more well-ordered trucks, especially from organizations with as much money and clout as the Boy Scouts. We began to make slow progress in offloading the mess and made small talk to distract ourselves from the early heat of the day.

"Do you know the Boy Scouts have more pedophiles than the Catholic Church?" Will asked after a while, not realizing how relevant his words were.

"I'm not surprised," I said, "And those pompous bastards think that excluding gays from their ranks proves their morality."

Will looked up at me, surprised, and wiped his forehead with his sleeve.

"Sounds like you've got a beef with them."

I shrugged, even though he couldn't see me as he bent to pick up another box.

"No, not really."

We continued working in silence, but my internal dialogue was getting fired up just thinking about it. The Boy Scouts had been in the news that summer as they reaffirmed their stance on banning gay members and volunteers. Still, I hadn't paid much attention to the headlines at the time or allowed myself to be moved by the obvious corruption implied in them. Somehow, Will's comments and the answering burst of feeling they raised in me called the issue to the forefront of my consciousness. I'd spent enough time in therapy over the past years to know that when these feelings surfaced it was best to face them.

"What's with all this junk anyway?" I asked, tossing a box out of the truck with a bit more force than I had intended. "Are they suddenly poor?"

"Are you kidding? Not by a long shot. They've got millions. They're an organization that thrives on volunteers."

The rest of the morning passed uneventfully. We finished the job and I began heading home in the early evening. The sunset over the desert was majestic and I appreciated the broad strokes of burnt-orange and subtle wisps of purple with as much awe as ever. But my mind was in turmoil. Ever since my conversation with Will, I felt something nagging at me. On the long drive home, I thought about what he'd said and about my own reaction. The more I thought about it, the more I felt the overwhelming injustice of it all. Here was this massive institution—the Boy Scouts of America—sitting on millions of dollars and claiming righteousness when so many young men out there had had their lives irrevocably damaged by the pedophiles that they seemingly did little to discourage. I knew from experience that the Mormon Church was no better. It was a powerful puppeteer and the shattered lives of a few individuals are easily overlooked when you're pulling as many strings as they are. For all the good these organizations did—I was suddenly certain— they were responsible for an equal or greater amount of bad. When would the balance finally tip? When would the harm done outweigh their power and greed?

My anger mounted as I suddenly confronted what I'd clearly been ignoring for some time. The thing is, when you live the kind of life I'd led, there are so many issues to face that it's never easy to go back and say, "*There* is where it all began." Sometimes you can't see the trunk of the tree for all the branches that obscure it. God knows I had enough of these derivative issues to keep my therapists employed for life. All this time I'd been clearing branches, but I would never be able to cut the tree down until I got at the source. And now I felt that it was suddenly staring me in the face, and it was one hell of a monstrous beast to fell.

Throughout the following week, I talked incessantly about nothing else with whoever would listen. I spent many a waking hour on the computer, researching the statute of limitations on sexual abuse cases in the state of California, where my own tragedy took place. I quickly realized that California was one of the worst possible states to bring forward a case like mine in. Victims had until their 28th birthday to file a case against a childhood sex abuse. Still, I caught a tantalizing glimpse of something on the periphery. I read that there were many proponents pushing to get a bill before Congress that would extend this statute of limitations for the span of one year. This was the faint glimmer of hope that was to become SB-131, a bill that would allow so many silent survivors to have their cases brought before a court, and I chose to hitch my own hopes to it. The more I delved into the various issues pertaining to my case, the more inspired I became and the more certain that it was time to seek justice for the great wrong that had been done to me. And the sex abuse itself was just a drop in the bucket compared to the larger issue.

In my desire to seek justice at last, Arlene was my greatest ally. She was born a fighter and she too had been through a significant amount of trauma in her life. In our desire to live in the light and do the right thing, we were not to be daunted. I filled an entire legal notepad in the days after the convention with a flood of ideas as I purged myself of the pent up need for retribution. As I did so, the anger faded. I felt peace return and the issue resolved itself plainly on the page. This was nothing more than an issue of right and wrong. And I was taking it before the supreme authority of black and white morality: the Mormon Church.

The following day I sent the letter that would preface one of the most difficult years of my life. In it, I leveled my complaint of sexual abuse against the Church of Jesus Christ of Latter Day Saints and The Boy Scouts of America. The incidents, I explained, began in 1983 at the Northridge First Ward in Northridge, California and continued for many months. I further detailed the horrors that took place. The manipulation, the torture, the degradation that I endured at the hands of Scoutmaster Craig Mathias. What I could not explain in words was the confusion and resounding pain and self-loathing that set my life on a downward spiral for so many years after. I'd had dreams of playing major league baseball as a boy, but instead my life took a dramatically different turn. How could I hope to make the Church understand such a thing? They hadn't understood at the time of these events. My father and I reported the incidents shortly after they happened to Bishop Brent Griffiths. He discounted my credibility as nicely as he could and directed the focus of that meeting on my own misdeeds.

Five years later, in 1987, Craig Mathias was convicted of sexually abusing five boy scouts just up the road in Canyon Country. I made all of this plain in the letter, how I believed these crimes could have been prevented had my own claims been taken seriously. Since then I'd researched similar cases to my own. I found some startling evidence. I researched cases in which Tim Kosnoff in Seattle, Washington, and Kelly Clark of Portland, Oregon stated that the Church of Jesus Christ of Latter Day Saints tried to deal with such cases "in house." I laid it all out, but there was still so much more to say.

In writing the letter, I sought the council of my good friend Paul and we debated for a long time over how much compensation I should ask for. After finding it nearly impossible to put a value on twenty-nine years of pain and suffering, we decided not to include a number at all. Later, I was glad that I did this. It would force the hand of the opposing council to determine the value of their own negligence.

CHAPTER TWO

1980-1983

From down the street, I heard my dad calling my name.

"Aw, shit," I said, "The old man's calling me in."

"Maybe you can ignore him. Pretend you're too far away to hear," one of the neighbor boys said.

"Nah," I said, hurtling the last pebble into the tree in his backyard where we'd been trying to scare birds away. "I have to go."

I was reluctant to stop playing with my friends, but I was even less interested in having my dad come find me. Then my friends would find out why I had to leave and I didn't like being known as a cub scout, a church boy.

I walked slowly home, kicking stones and swinging a stick. When I got within range of my house, I saw my dad waiting on the front stoop, already buttoned into his scouting shirt.

"Do I have to go?" I whined, slinking up the driveway.

"You know the answer to that."

My dad put a hand on my back and guided me inside.

"Go suit up. I'll be waiting," he said.

I was less than willing to be dragged away from my

friends and herded off to Cub Scouts, but once I was there it was always a good time. I liked having my dad as a Scoutmaster since he was a pretty fun guy and I liked spending time with him camping and hiking, or even just tying knots and learning about knives and rifles. As I got dressed that day, I began to feel excited remembering that we would be preparing for the Pinewood Derby Race taking place that weekend. By the time I was ready to go, I bounded out of my room saying, "Dad, we have to finish getting the car ready!"

"We will, we will. But right now we need to leave or we'll be late. Say good-bye to your mom."

"Bye mom!" I called but the door was already shut behind me when I heard her faint voice replying, "Bye, Tommy. I love you."

All of our scouting meetings were held mid-week at the same Mormon church we attended every Sunday. That year they were adding a new building onto the church, facing Plummer Street, and we were barely out of the car before the building dust began to settle over the contours of the car. I ran ahead of my dad, eager now to meet up with Max and Sean, my best buddies in church and Scouts. Max Harding was somewhat reserved and might have been a loner had it not been for me and Sean bringing out the best—or possibly worst—in him. Together the three of us were always getting into one type of mischief or another, all in good fun. The grown-ups loved us but had a hard time keeping us still in meetings and especially in church.

The meeting played out as they all did and I hardly believed it when it was time to leave. I was a busy kid and always invested fully in activities when they were interesting enough to capture my attention. At the age of ten, I was easily caught up in the prospect of building and racing my Pinewood Derby car. Sean and Max and I left the scout meeting chatting animatedly about our certain victory in the coming race.

When the weekend came, the day of the event dawned bright and full of possibility. Before heading out, my dad and I checked our car to make sure that all of the fresh paint we'd put on the night before was dry and ready to go. We loaded up and headed out for the church. The scouts quickly gathered into their respective packs and I was eager to show off my car to the other guys. My mom and brothers arrived later in the morning and milled around with the rest of the church folk who'd come to join in the fun. I saw my sisters, too, who were with their friends.

At last it was our turn to race. I was certain my car was a winner and I put it on the starting line feeling quite proud. The next few minutes passed in a haze of excitement. Me and the rest of the boys were jumping up and down and cheering on our cars until, moments later, they crossed the finish line. It was a close finish and I turned to my dad yelling, "I won! I think I won!"

"Well, let's listen for the final announcement," he said and clapped me on the shoulder.

I hopped anxiously from one foot to another and it seemed like an eternity before the winner was announced and sure enough, I had done it. My car had won! I was elated. Max and Sean both gave me high-fives and several of the other boys congratulated me. I beamed with pride as my mom snapped off a picture. I could hardly believe it, but at the same time it was exactly as I'd imagined it. All through the rest of the day, I talked about that race and replayed the events ceaselessly for anyone who would listen.

The next day was a church day. The excitement of the

race hadn't worn off, and the last thing I wanted to do was be cooped up in church all morning. I grumbled about having to get ready, even while the older kids, Tina, Margie, and Tim, were getting in the car. My mom carried the baby, Dennis, and pulled little David along by the hand. But I was on my own, tugging at the buttons on my shirt and vocalizing my dissatisfaction for all to hear.

"Come on, Tommy. I'm sure there are a few people at church who haven't heard the story of your big win yet," my dad said, smirking.

I always attended church with some amount of reluctance. The church was like a stern and disapproving father. For my parents, this had been a welcome force in their lives. As the children of alcoholic parents, they had both longed for stability and a loving, nurturing home life which they did a good job of providing for us kids. I've heard that when he suggested it to my mother she was not entirely on board. My dad was researching religions and someone gave him a book on Mormonism. My mother turned down the idea. But in the end, her craving for something wholesome and didactic to believe in must have won out. Her initial rejection of the idea struck me as somehow false, since in all the time that I've known her she has been nothing but vigilant in her devotion to all things church related.

My dad was gentle and forgiving. He was a hard-working man, but also loving. From our house off Sepulveda Boulevard, in Northridge, he drove south to Hollywood where he worked in the film labs, on optical and special effects. It was good, steady work and he was a good, steady man who still found time to lead my Cub Scout troop. Neither of my parents were ever idle. They were always working; restless in a way that only those who have faced true hardship can be. My mother's friends always commented on how nice it must be to have a husband who completed so much work around the house without ever having to be asked.

Church that day was no different from any other. I sat snickering with my friends until my parents called me to sit with them. During the service, I found sitting still to be the hardest thing. Once in a while, my dad would take sympathy on me and lean over to whisper something funny about one of the other ward members and I would try to stifle a laugh. This often got me riled up and I'd push the limit too far before both parents signaled me with a look that it was time to get it under control. Still, those were happy times.

Soon my dad had to take on an additional job to help support the family and he was no longer able to participate in my scouting activities. By then I was growing older anyways and often preferred not to have my dad around enforcing the limits that my buddies and I were only interested in pushing. I became less and less interested in going to Boy Scouts and it was a constant struggle between my parents and me. They were masters at striking a bargain with a wily boy on the verge of becoming a teenager. If I argued against going to church, they would say, "Well, you can skip church this week, but at least go to Boy Scouts." If I fought them on going to a Boy Scout meeting, they would threaten to remove the Ozzy and Motley Crue posters from my wall. So I always went.

In 1983, when I was thirteen, a new Scoutmaster was assigned to our troop. We all knew him as he'd been raised up in the church and had been a leader in other troops. His name was Craig Mathias and he was as uninteresting as a saltine cracker. By that time I was more interested in hanging out with Max, Sean, and Max's older brother Andy than in scouting. Only weeks before this, I had tried marijuana with them for the first time and realized that all of the fear my dad and the church had tried to instill in me about the horrors of marijuana use had been useless chatter. Having conquered one of these fear-based doctrines, I felt invincible. I didn't realize then that these illusions of fearlessness concealed a great many insecurities.

The new Plummer Building had been completed and we had our own room in the west side of the building for Scout meetings. Down a long hallway and across from the basketball court, which also served as the cultural hall, we met each Wednesday night. After a few weeks, things started getting interesting. As the end of our meeting approached one night, Craig looked at the clock.

"We've got about twenty minutes to kill. You guys are all young, full of energy...who's interested in doing some physical fitness and getting stronger than all the other guys?"

We all must have been somewhat reluctant because he sweetened the deal. "All right, we'll make it fun, let's play Simon Says."

He had us line up. I was in the back with Max and Sean was in the front row.

"Simon says, do jumping jacks."

We all jumped.

"Stop."

Some of the guys stopped and they were out. Those of us who kept going stayed in the game.

"Simon says take off your shirt."

There were some snickers from the boys who'd just

departed the game. The rest of us paused. I was probably one of the first to take off my shirt, full of machismo and never one to turn down a dare. Some of the boys did the same, while a few others refused after much hemming and hawing, and opted out.

"Stop."

A few more boys went to the sidelines. I was one of three left.

"Simon says do push-ups."

We did.

"Pants down."

We laughed. Craig laughed.

"Well, then, tough guys. Simon says pants down."

We paused. Not to be outdone, I lowered my pants. The rest of the group laughed at my boldness. The last one left in the game now, I was hamming it up.

"Okay, Simon says do jumping jacks."

After a goofy attempt at jumping jacks, with my pants around my ankles and the rest of the boys laughing, I finished with the charade and pulled up my jeans.

"All right, all right," Craig said, "So there's at least one of you who follows directions. That's it for today. I'll see you guys next week.

Looking back, I see clearly now that he was feeling us all out, seeing who would play along with his games and push the limits. I was not only more daring than some of the other boys, but also more curious. Thoughts of sexuality had been imbedded in me at an early age and so many issues regarding its propriety lay guarded in the recesses of my mind. So much so that I didn't realize, at the age of thirteen, that they were there. The incident in my childhood was like a hazy dream, involving another time, another place, and another little boy.

Even now, I see it play out as if I'm on the outside looking in. My mother was in the kitchen doing dishes; a disconnected form behind the glass. I was in the yard, playing with the kittens. My older sisters and brother were at school, the younger ones hadn't been born yet, so I was used to playing on my own during the day. As a five-year-old, I loved those kittens and I must have been giving them all of my attention. I didn't see the stranger drifting up the street. I turned around and he was standing there. He waved at me. He was fat and sweaty, with graying hair and a rough, two-week beard. When I think of him standing there, it fills me with darkness. But as a little boy I had no concept of the evils man is capable of. I saw only a smile and a friendly wave. My mother was just there, in the kitchen. If I was wrong, surely she would know it.

"Do you want to see my kittens?"

The next thing I remember, I was floating outside of my body, fifteen feet away and watching myself from an angle. I was on the side of the house, performing oral sex on this man, my friend.

Francis, a creepy guy who lived across the street and was always policing the neighborhood, happened to pass by his window and by some miracle, looked out. He was the one to call the police. I did not understand what I had done wrong, or why the police came and took the man away. Later, when I had to testify in court, I finished giving my testimony and was being led out of the courtroom.

"Wait," I said, "What about my friend?"

"Oh, Tommy, he's not your friend. He was using you. He's not a good man or a friend to you."

I didn't understand this. Using me for what? I had no money, nothing he wanted. I was just a kid.

"I want to see him. I have to say good-bye."

There was a long pause in which the grown-ups all looked at each other, assessing the risk as if such things can be measured and damages calculated in simple terms. In the end I was allowed to see him. I walked over to where he sat, behind bars. I waved at him and he waved back.

"See you pal," I said.

The only thing I knew was that I had done something wrong and that he and I were in it together. If he was bad, maybe I was too.

Weeks went by and Craig played his little games with us. At one of the meetings we were all quieter than usual and Craig picked up on the fact that we were lacking in our usual energy.

"Did you know that hypnotism can be used to cure almost any problem?" he asked us. "I learned all about performing hypnotism and I used to have a hard time waking up in the morning. I know you guys have the same problem, right?"

There were a few nods.

"Well, I hypnotized myself and now I don't even set an alarm clock. I wake up at the same time every day and I don't even feel tired. That's what hypnotism can do for you. We can try it sometime. You'll be amazed."

An accountant by trade, he was a careful, methodical man. His approach was seamless. Of course I was interested in his claim that he could perform hypnotism. To think that a person could change their life, their will, and possibly the will of others? This was a tantalizing trick to a boy who wanted to bend the rules. A natural salesman, he could pick up on our weaknesses and play to them without ever appearing overly forceful. He had a full bag of tricks and if he suggested another round of Simon Says but we were more interested in Truth or Dare, he was always willing to change it up and try another tactic.

One night I went to church after smoking weed for the second time and he must have noticed that something was off. He asked if I would stay after the rest of the boys left. The first thing that crossed my mind was, *Oh, shit. He's going to try and give me grief about this. But what can he do? He's just a stupid Scoutmaster. I don't give a fuck about Scouts anyway.*

When the rest of the boys were gone, I was surprised by how quiet it felt, like we were the only two people in the building. Suddenly, I was vulnerable and I hated him in that moment for making me feel like a kid who was about to get reprimanded.

"I just wanted to tell you," he began, "that I think I can understand some of what you're going through. I know you get in trouble and I've been in my share of trouble, too. You might think I'm going to chew you out for getting high, but smoking marijuana is nothing new to me. I've been in trouble for it before. I just wanted you to know that you can talk to me about anything, okay?"

I was surprised and he saw it on my face. I was never any good at lying or hiding my emotions. I was an easy read. Another night, he asked me how long I'd been smoking. Feeling that I could trust him not to tell my parents or turn me in, I told him I'd only done it twice. With the lines of communication open, it was easy after that to divulge my struggles to him. I told him I didn't know why I always got in trouble. I just felt like I couldn't do anything right.

"You think you've been in trouble? I got in so much trouble I had to be sent home from my mission," he laughed.

"Really? What did you do?"

"It's not important what I did. It's just important that the church overlooked it and let me alone. Now I can hang out with guys like you and make a real difference."

I appreciated that. I was always interested in people who could relate to me; those who'd been around the block and gotten into trouble. I couldn't respect people who were overly righteous or who went around on a moral high-horse. At twenty-three, I figured this guy might at least remember and understand what it was to be in my shoes.

"Yeah, well I don't get off the hook so easy," I said. "I feel like if it's not my parents trying to tell me what to do, it's the church. Everyone wants to me sit and focus, but I can't. I can't be the way they want me to be."

"So, what is it that distracts you the most?"

"Girls." I laughed and Craig joined in.

"Yeah, well, if you want to please girls, I can help you with that."

My dad was working a lot, so it fell to my mom to be in charge of most things that had to do with us kids. It was easy for Craig to pull her aside and tell her that the reason I was staying late so many nights was that he'd gotten me to open up to him and he felt he could help me with some of my teenage waywardness. My mom was more than willing to accept this. She knew I was dealing with the things that many boys in their early teens go through and it must have appealed to her to have someone from the church taking an interest in me.

It began that way. He told me that his friends at Granada High School had nicknamed him the "Egg Man" like the Beatles song because he always brought hard-boiled eggs when they were getting high. Had it not been for my unresolved questions about the sexual encounter I'd had when I was a boy, I might not have given in. As it was, I didn't fully understand what Craig had in mind, but I was pleased with the attention. My friends and I bonded over getting in trouble together. Here was someone who wanted to bond with me in a different way—by helping me. Deep down, that was all I wanted; to heal the pain and residual confusion of a traumatic encounter. To understand the effects and to understand who I was, in a context other than the coldness of church or the closeness of family. Here was a friend, offering just what I needed.

But the help he gave quickly melded into something more. Who was I to reject his assurances that he understood me and knew what I needed? When he suggested that we get naked, so he could show me how sexuality could be a good thing, something in me was repulsed by the idea. But something else in me wanted to know more. I didn't know where the lines were because they'd been erased so long ago. Manual intercourse was the easiest. He told me that if I learned how it felt to be pleased, and to please another, I would have no trouble with girls. This happened in that same room in the back of the Plummer Building where all of our meetings took place. I was disgusted at first, but tried to tell myself that it was helping me. Then before we left he said, "I want to show you something."

I buttoned my pants and watched as he took a pencil from his shirt. His khakis were still undone and his cock was hanging out. He took it in one hand and began to shove the lead tip into the head of his penis. I cringed and looked away.

"No," he said, "I want you to look. I want you to see the power of hypnotism. I've gotten to a point where I no longer have to feel pain. You can do away with your pain

24

too, Tommy. I can show you how."

When he wanted me to go to his house, my mother had no qualms about it. She was certain that his status as a Mormon was enough to get him into heaven and surely what was good enough for God was good enough for me. I doubt now that my father knew much about Craig's influence in my life. My mother had a way of keeping little things from him. I would often get in trouble and convince her not to tell my dad. Whether it was in his best interests or even intentional on her part, I'm sure it was easier for Mom to just tell him us kids were doing church activities than to relay the details of our comings and goings. I only think this may have been the case because I found out much later that my dad had his own reasons to suspect that Brother Mathias's intentions were less than wholesome, and I wonder if he might have limited our interactions had he known of the time we spent together.

I was less than eager to spend time alone with Craig because a large part of me was still alarmed by what was happening. But I knew that he lived with his mother and sister, and that his house was an informal meeting place where we scouts could go and somehow this made me feel that nothing would happen if I didn't want it to.

The first time I went to his house his mother and sister were there. Craig said he wanted to talk about what had happened. He said he wanted to show me more. He could open my eyes to penetration and how good it could feel.

"I'm into girls, though...I don't..."

My feeble attempts to ward him off were nothing against the powers of persuasion.

"I know you are, but you can have any girl, if you just

do what I show you."

He had us take turns performing oral sex, which was better than masturbation if I closed my eyes and tried hard to visualize myself elsewhere. Then he performed anal sex on me and nothing in it was enjoyable in the least.

"Now, if you do it on me you'll see the difference. It will be just like doing it on a girl. Close your eyes, you'll see."

I'd kissed girls before, and had even managed to cop a feel once or twice with some of the friendlier girls at school. It was somewhat easier to imagine that I was laying any one of them down and having my way. But when it was over, I felt sick. Instead of making me feel closer or more connected to anyone or anything, these episodes were beginning to make me feel even further away. This, I understand, is the way predators isolate their pray. As twisted as his role was in initiating these events, he was the only one who understood this messed up situation I was in. If I stopped it, I would have been completely alone.

One afternoon, I tried to leave after the meeting with the other boys but Craig intervened.

"Tommy, you boys made a mess in the bathroom earlier. Come clean it up real quick and then you can go."

It was true that some of the other kids and I had been messing around in the bathroom, but he and I both knew this was not the real reason why he detained me. By then I knew I couldn't refuse him, though. I didn't want the other boys to find out what was happening. Silence was a better option. I went along with it and followed him to the bathroom across the hall from our meeting room. There was a lock on the door and he engaged it.

"You remember what I showed you after the last meeting? With the pencil?"

I nodded.

"I want you to try it, but I've found something that will make it easier for you."

He pulled out a matchstick. I froze. He proceeded to torture my genitals with the blunt end of the stick, trying to force it into the opening of my urethra. I squeezed my eyes shut and tried to hold still, willing it to be over. There was no pleasure, no illusion that I could draw from the experience to shield myself with. The pain was excruciating and I told him I wanted to stop. He pulled back. He showed me again how easy it was for him and asked me, didn't I want to be hypnotized and try to do it again, painlessly?

Seeing as how the door was locked and I had little choice in the matter, I agreed that he could hypnotize me. Anything was better than the pain he inflicted. On the drone of his words, I tried hard to slip into some alternate reality, some place where there would be freedom from feeling. Nothing happened. When he was done, I pretended to be hypnotized. I clenched my jaws shut tight as he pulled out a pencil this time. I told him if I had to do it I'd prefer he use the eraser end. He must have felt he was obliging me when he tried to insert the pencil eraser into my penis. If I pretended, I thought, he might let me go sooner.

My sister Margie was the same age as Craig and she knew of him. Margie was always a fun, pretty girl and she told me a strange story once about Craig's father. The Mathias family had a catamaran and my sister went on the boat for a church outing years before Craig was introduced to me. They were to be spending the night on the boat, and when they'd been on board for a while, Mr. Mathias, who everyone called Captain, came out to where all the kids were and said, "Okay, I've put everyone's names in a hat and we're going to draw them one by one to see who will be sleeping with who tonight." Since there were boys and girls on the trip, this didn't sit well with the kids, who rejected the idea of possibly having to bed up with a member of the opposite sex. But Margie said the Captain gave her the creeps and he continued to be much too interested in the sleeping arrangements.

Margie was always one to be vocal in her opposition of whatever agenda our parents had for her. They were always schlepping us kids around and making us do things we didn't want to. One of Margie's jobs when she was in her early teens was babysitting. At the end of the night, she was often driven home by the dads of the kids she sat for. Margie told our mom she didn't want to babysit for one of the families anymore because the dad gave her the creeps. Instead of listening to her though, my mom just said, "Oh, Margie, stop it. You're being ridiculous. They're a good church family and he's a good dad." It was her way, to brush things off completely; to turn a blind eye on the uncomfortable, unmentionable, or unthinkable. She is a loving mother and a great woman, but she has always seemed closed minded about the harsher ways of the world.

Since no one else saw that there was anything wrong with the time I spent with Craig, it was hard not to let it happen. Surely if it was so wrong the grown-ups would discover it and put a stop to it? On the last occasion that I visited his house, Craig's mother and younger sister were home again, but I already knew this would make no difference in what he was willing to try. We went to his room and he shut the door. His mother was a thin, frail woman compared to her large and looming husband. My dad had always kept the Captain at arm's length, since he was a rather intimidating guy. Compared to him, his wife was sullen and rather quiet.

With his mother and sister in the same house, I was surprised when Craig began to masturbate me. I made my usual, feeble attempt at stopping, but I have to confess that at the age of thirteen, when one's genitals are being stimulated it's very hard to know what to do; what's right or what's wrong. He tried to hypnotize me again and, thankful that I could have a few moments of peace, I went along with it. In the middle of this there was a knock at the door.

"Craig?" his mother called, with concern in her voice, "Is everything okay?"

"Yeah, Mom, we're just talking. Give us a minute."

That slight tremble in her voice was the first sign I had that what was happening was wrong. It didn't do much, it wasn't like we had to stop. Things dragged out a little longer. But hearing the care in her voice provided a gauge for me and for the first time I saw things not from the inside looking out, but from the outside looking in. It was that slight nudge that I needed, the small wedge of doubt that maybe Craig didn't know me like he said, and maybe he was not truly helping me.

Since then, I have heard that same tone from my mother many times. That same Mormon concern. Later, when I'd have girls over and shut the door, my mother would knock in the same way, calling my name with that same panicky tremor in her voice. But there's a difference between worrying and taking action. So often we don't step forward to stop something when doing so would be difficult. It's so much easier to tell ourselves we've done enough, or convince ourselves that nothing is really wrong

29

when it is. We put forth these half-hearted attempts at confronting the situation, hoping we won't have to deal with it or acknowledge it; hoping the problem will resolve itself and go away. So often it's easier to leave the door shut.

The following month, Craig mentioned that he was thinking of organizing a Disneyland trip. I told him it sounded fun. He didn't bring it up in our meetings and I soon forgot. Then my mom mentioned that he'd talked to her about it. I can only imagine the slickness with which he convinced her. No doubt he played on the usefulness of helping a young boy forget the cares of the world for a day.

"I don't think I'll go," I said when my mom brought it up.

"I think you should. Don't worry about the money, it sounds like it will be fun for you."

I told Craig that maybe we could go another time.

"Oh. Well I was going to ask some of the other boys to go, too."

"Well, then maybe…"

When he came to pick me up, he was alone. My mom stood at the door, smiling at him. I felt a resentful dread settle in the pit of my stomach. The wolf had come to call and there was nothing I could do but go with. Feeling entirely alone and forsaken, I got in the car and sat quietly while Craig chattered away on the drive to Disneyland. Not even my initial excitement to visit the theme park was enough to make that ride enjoyable.

After a while, he reached over and fondled me through my pants, "Come on, cheer up. What do I have to do?"

"Nothing. I'm okay."

In another mile or two, he pulled off the road and leaned into me. He kissed me and continued to fondle me, trying to get inside my pants. Never had I felt so out of control in my life. I was trapped in a car with no way out of the situation. Before, I had always felt that there was at least some chance, however small, that I could avoid him if I had to. There was at least the illusion of free will. Now I was being propelled forward by the machinations of this man, forced to keep this horrific secret, because what could I do now to save myself? How would I ever find a way out?

Convinced that if I just let him do what he wanted to do it would soon be over, the day passed with nightmarish unreality. Once at Disneyland, I was no safer than in the car. Craig molested me on the rides when he could and I dreaded entering those darkened realms with him. I longed to stay in the sunlight, among the throngs of people, where I imagined I might vanish invisibly among them at any moment. Where Craig had once played on my insecurities and made me believe he was the only one who understood me, now his every advance became an assurance to me that he did not.

While I wanted to leave the park, I dreaded the ride home. When the time came, I endured his actions again by absenting myself from my mind and looking at some place in the future where things made sense and where the lines between right and wrong were clear and it was easy and worthwhile to trust. I made a vow to myself that if I made it through that day, it would be the last time I allowed myself to be alone with Craig. And it was.

At around that time, the church assigned an Assistant Scoutmaster to our troop. Whether this was due to any specific concerns about Craig's behavior or was simply a matter of policy, it was long past due. They'd let Craig

Mathias slink around unchecked for far too long. Soon after he joined us, Michael Morring and Craig began to plan our annual summer camp event for the following month.

I'd been to Camp Whitsett once before and I was excited for this event. When the day finally arrived to set out on the trip, Max and Sean and I sat in the back of one of the vans that was charged with driving us all to the camp. Free from our parents for a week, we must have felt like the world was our oyster. We were full of plans and ideas for how to make the most out of the camp experience. In our excitement, we may have gotten slightly carried away.

One of the lifeguards at the camp was a big, athletic guy named Chris Purvis. It was not a huge leap for us to begin calling him "Purvis the Pervert" behind his back. The previous year I had gone to camp and the older boys called him that. It was never to his face of course, because they all actually respected him. But when my turn at camp came I was excited to do the same thing the older boys had done because it made me cool. This had more to do with an indiscriminate adolescent sense of humor than it had to do with the man himself. Chris was a nice guy and far from being an actual pervert. We all thought he was really cool. One night, we were in our sleeping bags on our bunks and in the excited delirium typical of young boys who have had too little sleep and too much freedom, we began to execute a plan that we knew would land us in a lot of trouble if we were caught.

That night, we posted large, pink signs throughout the camp that proclaimed: "Purvis is a Pervert." We waited for chaos to ensue. Sure enough, the following morning the camp was in an uproar. The kids all thought it was funny for about five minutes before they saw the looks on the faces of the leaders and realized the hammer might fall on them if they enjoyed the spectacle too much. I wondered then how I was pinpointed as the culprit behind those signs, but I realize now that my own reaction was probably a dead giveaway. In our determination to appear innocent, we must have made ourselves conspicuous. As it was, camp went on without any accusations made and no disciplinary action taken.

I began to feel invincible. Especially when, the following night, Craig tried to hypnotize several of us boys and suggested that to do so we must get naked in our sleeping bags.

"What are you talking about?" Michael Morring intervened, "You can't do that."

He was a puzzled kind of guy and wasn't one to lay down the law, but he clearly scratched his head at this.

"Tommy will do it, won't you?" Craig said, turning to me to act as an example for the rest.

The last thing I wanted was to be singled out. Realizing that with Michael's presence there I didn't have to go along with this, I declined.

Returning home from camp, I thought I was free and clear. Then, the day after I got home, the phone rang. It was the Bishop and he requested a meeting with me and my parents. My dad agreed that he would take me to the meeting and asked me, in an exasperated voice, what I'd done now. In my head, the alarms were going off. I was scared and I knew that my dad would be pissed when he found out what I'd done. It was fun to cause a little trouble, but I always failed to overlook how little joy adults often got out of my antics.

When we arrived at the Bishop's office in the main

church, he called us in. When the door opened, I immediately saw the sign. A perfect, photographed copy of the pink "Purvis is a Pervert" sign lay in the middle of the Bishop's desk. Bishop Brent Griffiths was a beet red guy and when he was angry, he got even redder. His face was positively fuchsia as he met my eyes over that damning piece of evidence. *Shit, shit, shit,* I thought, and my insides trembled. My dad and I sat down in the chairs that faced the Bishop's desk. Dad let out a prolonged sigh as he sat and I saw that his eyes were on the sign. They both looked at me and Bishop Griffith's began to give an accounting of my actions that did nothing to improve his color. I hung my head.

Then the questions came. Had I been involved? I shrugged. Did I realize the seriousness of publicly calling someone a pervert? I nodded. Did I know that I was wrong? Yes. Did I regret the humiliation I'd caused Mr. Purvis? Yes.

"You have embarrassed the church and stained our image! Are you proud of that?"

The Bishop's color rose. Then, because part of me was already angry at the Bishop and the Church for condemning me when they were blind to the real evil in their midst, and partly to get myself out of trouble, I mumbled, "What if it was the truth?"

Bishop Griffiths was brought up short.

"What do you mean?"

"What if it was true…about someone?"

"Who?"

I shrugged.

"About who, Tommy?"

"Well…about Craig. He does weird stuff with the kids."

34

Bishop Griffiths finally moved. He sat up straight and leaned back in his chair.

"What kind of 'weird stuff?'"

"I dunno. Like making them get naked and doing other stuff."

Leaning forward again, the Bishop puffed himself up like a balloon. "Tommy," he said in his most Bishop-y voice, "I want you to know that you are making some very serious accusations here."

At the same time, my dad said, "Did he do these things to you?"

Keeping my head down, I nodded. This seemed to deflate Bishop Griffiths. His voice had less force when he said, "I want you to think about what you're saying, Tommy."

"Tell the Bishop what happened, Tom."

"Just...bad stuff. Touching, I guess, and...other things."

Suddenly, I wanted to be anywhere but in that room saying the things I was saying. I didn't want to talk about it. I wanted it to be over.

My dad looked at the Bishop and the two were silent for several moments. Then the Bishop regained his composure.

"Well, I'll look into it. You just worry about the stuff you've done here," he tapped the sign, "and we'll worry about the rest."

Walking out of the church, my dad and I were both silent. I felt as distant from him as I'd ever felt. In the car, we said nothing and after a while he flipped the radio on. In another moment he turned it down again.

"That stuff really happen?" he asked.

"Yeah."

I can't blame him. He didn't know what to do. I didn't either. It was easier to mull it over in silence, each on our own.

Many years later, I learned that my dad called the Bishop later in the week and asked what was being done about Craig. Bishop Griffith's said they were trying to get him in so they speak with him, but he wasn't cooperating.

"Well, go get him and bring him in yourself then!" my dad said.

There were a few more phone calls, a few more delays. Craig must have sensed that it was all coming down on him because he stopped showing up to our Scout meetings. Michael Morring scrambled to organize us and became our unofficial Scoutmaster in his absence. After that day in the Bishop's office, Craig was just gone. I never learned if he got removed or if he just chose to move on, but I gathered from my dad's accounts that the church was never able to call him in or address the issues I'd raised. If they had, things might have turned out differently. It was several years before I would learn where Craig went and how a single failure to take action could tragically alter the lives of so many. As it was, that afternoon in the Bishop's office might never have happened. Nothing was done. No one spoke of it. My report didn't even make it into the unkempt records at the Boy Scout headquarters in Irving, Texas, which were later made public on October 18, 2012, in a landmark scandal. The church brushed it off like an annoying fleck of lint from a clean white shirt.

CHAPTER THREE

1983-1985

Dear Gina,

Sitting in this congregation is killing me. I feel like a huge, open sore sitting in this pew. Why do these people all appear to have no problems? All I need is a little relief from the thousands of problems hot on my heels and I'm sure as fuck not getting any here.

Behind the stage at the front of the church there are windows on both sides. When I look out of the left window, it's the only thing between freedom and me. This is crazy. This place is a prison and I'm locked up with a hundred happy people. They're not even real! I'd probably be better off in a real prison, or with my real friend Andy in Sylmar Juvy.

Maybe I really am the seed of the devil, or at least possessed by him. This music I'm listening to is perfect. Iron Maiden, Number of the Beast. Black Sabbath, We Sold Our Soul for Rock 'n' Roll. Motley Crue, Too Fast for Love. I take to it, like a fish to water. How I feel is the only real thing; the only thing worth following in life. Everyone sitting around me is fucking fake. Maybe this is my purpose...to be the only genuine person in a room full of hypocrites and liars...

With the truth finally told and Craig gone, it was as if none of it had ever happened. For everyone but me, that is. For me it was as if the door was shut and everyone was on the other side, hardly realizing I was gone. Meanwhile, I stumbled through the darkness in a silent place. I learned to rely on my senses, feeling my way through life without a compass or a guide.

Andy Harding was Max's older brother and I hung out a lot with him. He was outspoken and seemed so strong. He didn't put up with a lot of shit and I did. I admired him and wanted to be more like him. Andy introduced me to a guy named Ted who lived in Sylmar and we hung out with him sometimes. Ted's dad grew weed and always had a good supply on hand. I knew now that marijuana wasn't the great evil that I'd been preached against. Instead, it simplified everything. Life was easy when we were smoking out all afternoon at Ted's house and I was cast adrift and untethered to anything. It was how I wanted it, or how I needed it, maybe. Sometimes there were girls around, but they weren't there for me. Still, I hung around Andy and Ted while the girls were drawn to their long hair and an easily procured high, and I'd hope somehow one of them would accidentally like me.

When I was left to my own devices, I missed that easy letting go that came with a good smoke, so I bought cigarettes and raided the medicine cabinet at home for cough syrup or anything that would get me drowsy and let me slip once more into the warm embrace of forgetfulness. I hung out with some of the boys in the neighborhood and we rode bikes or skateboards and played sports. My dad taught me to play baseball years before and I was a good ball player, athletic and coordinated. It came natural to me and I loved little league, although my interest was starting to fall away.

There was a rougher bunch of kids that lived at the end of the street, closer to Sepulveda Boulevard. Isaiah Gonzalez was half-black, half-Mexican. Ken Jensen was a big white kid with a strong demeanor, and his little brother Jamie was small and cute with an adventurous spirit. The girls already loved Jamie. Tony Garcia was the guy with all the ideas.

Across the street from us on the cul-de-sac, Jason Bowman's mom was dying of cancer. Jason was an only child and the same age as me. I was used to having brothers and I treated him no different than I treated them. His dad sometimes tossed a football around with us outside but he had sad eyes and his breath smelled of alcohol at any time of day. One day Isaiah told me he'd gotten a bag of weed off of Jason and I was pissed.

"Man, what are you doing giving Isaiah weed? Is it just because he sweated you out? You don't have to do that. Not when you're holding out on me. I live across the street from you, Jason!"

"Alright, I guess I can get you some, too."

Jason introduced me to the hefty bag of medical marijuana that was always available in his house and smoking it was a big step up from the homegrown that I could sit around and smoke for a whole afternoon. Getting high in my own neighborhood made things a lot easier. It also made the time that I spent in school and with my parents that much harder to bear. I had no interest in being in school, or in being told what to do in general. I couldn't understand how my parents understood me so little. Every command from them to do better in school, do my homework, or go to church was a direct insult to my free will. Every time they tried to talk to me about how I was wasting my potential or not trying hard enough, it only reinforced my belief that I was a disappointment to them and that I could do nothing right.

Then, one Sunday morning we were all at home and I was messing around with my brothers and watching TV; doing anything I could to avoid getting ready for dreaded church. Suddenly there was a frantic pounding on the front door. I jumped in my seat and looked out the front window that had a view of the porch. I recognized the woman who stood there looking over her shoulder and panting like she'd run a marathon. I'd seen her once in a while and knew she didn't live far from us. I also knew my dad kept her more than an arm's length away.

My dad answered the door with my mother not far behind. Ours was a quiet neighborhood and a crazy woman beating on the door was a sight to be seen for us kids. We all crowded around, trying to hear what was happening. My mom shooed us back and told us that Dad was dealing with it. We quieted and tried to listen, but all we could glean were the incoherent rantings of Aunt Cheryl, broken intermittently by Dad's calm, unaffected voice. Then she tried to push past him.

"...niggers after me!" she shouted. "...fucking monsters...they're all dead!"

I peered through the window again and saw my aunt's ugly, flat face contorted with fear. It was clear from her blank, staring eyes that she was out of her mind. We all looked at each other, our eyes huge and hands over our mouths to suppress those snickers that come with uneasy situations. Aunt Cheryl finally left and I watched her walk down the street as Dad came back inside and shut the door.

"What was that all about?" I asked.

"I don't know. She's on some hard drugs. She was hallucinating...thought there were monsters and black people chasing her. We don't need to talk any more about this. She's gone now and we need to get to church."

Far from being fearful of the situation and dropping it like everyone else did, I wanted to know more. I was curious about what had happened to Aunt Cheryl and why she was kept away. Even in these small and insignificant ways, I was drawn to the darkness that seemed to reside just on the fringes of my incomprehensible life. If I had so much trouble making sense of—and fitting into—my own life, maybe there was some relief to be found among the misunderstood outcasts of this world. Maybe there was some truth and belonging in those outer reaches.

The trouble I was getting into fueled my self-loathing, and this self-loathing became an identity of sorts. One thing perpetuated another and my life was like a stump with a wedge driven into it. Everything I did wrong and every complaint from my parents only drove the wedge in further until the fissure began to rupture on its own.

Nowhere was the consciousness of that wedge more prevalent than in the church. Nothing made me more aware of my worthlessness. It wasn't long before I fought my parents on attending church at every turn. But there was always a bargain to be struck. I was heavy into music by then, the darker the better. Recognizing this, my passion became an effective bargaining tool for my parents. My biggest role models at the time were Motley Crue. They lived eight miles away and were getting bigger and bigger all the time. My parents knew that the best way to motivate me was to threaten to take away music or offer me instruments and lessons in exchange for my obedience.

My parents, as much as we struggled to understand each other, were easy. They loved me and wanted the best for me and believed that I could be deterred from the path I was on. I struck a deal that year with my dad and agreed to attend church and try harder in school. In exchange, he rented me a guitar. At the ripe age of thirteen and fresh from a traumatic experience, I wanted nothing more than to lose myself in music and dreamed of being a rock star. Getting that guitar was well worth a stint of good behavior. Until I actually tried to play.

I felt like I was just bending the strings and trying to coax out something meaningful. Every incoherent note was a frustration of increasing magnitude until I finally tossed the instrument aside, convinced that every such failure was further evidence of my worthlessness. After that I was able to persuade my dad to take the guitar back and trade it for a set of drums. I knew I had to make this work. My parents had been hinting for some time that I could always go back to the piano and start with the basics. I couldn't go back to the fucking piano.

Drums ended up being more rewarding for someone like me, with little focus, no patience, and no formal training. I could see how to keep time and keep the beat, and learned to do some fills and riffs. I started taking lessons from the local music store. Music, however much I enjoyed it, was just another drug. I was too far gone by that point to be elevated by anything but the idea that I might someday find a way out of this life.

Sitting in my eighth grade classes, girls got most of my attention. But even on the topic of girls, my mind was drawn to darkness. I passed notes with some of them and to me it meant everything. Their minimal attention was equivalent to a declaration of love in my mind and to them it was probably just a playful way to pass the time. I thought if I could just get one girl and be with her and hold her, everything would be alright. But thoughts like these only fueled my self-hatred. If they really knew who I was and what I'd done they would be repulsed. They'd turn and run. Every time my attentions failed to manifest into sex, it was just more proof that there was something really wrong with me. Finally, I came to a solution.

I often sat in class; my pain and frustration festering. I thought how much better it would be if I were dead. I could show everyone! These girls would be sorry for not giving me action when they had a chance. That wacky church and my brainwashed parents would be sorry they'd fucked me up so badly. I started daydreaming about the possibility of killing myself and warmed to the idea. It was one of the only thoughts I had anymore that made me feel there might be a sense of justice in the world. Then I would look at my teacher and think, *I wonder what it would be like to toss her around?*

There was a black kid who sat near me in science class. He was bussed in from L.A. and he told me that he was involved in a gang. After class one day I stopped him in the hall.

"Do you know how I can get a gun?"

"What you want a gun for?"

"I just need to get one. Can you help me?"

He looked at me skeptically, then shrugged, "Yeah, I got plenty of 'em. I can get you one, but you can't tell nobody you got it from me."

I nodded. Every day after that I waited, fantasizing about how clean and easy it would be to blow my brains out; how sorry everyone else would be that they didn't listen or see my pain. There was a girl in a few of my classes named Suzanne Harrington and she had stringy blond hair and a nice butt. To me, she was the ultimate eighth grade girl. I was encouraged by the fact that she passed notes to me that always ended with a smiley face and a heart. This had to be the connection I was looking for.

We started talking here and there but I was only thinking of how I could get in her pants.

"Don't you want to come over sometime?" I'd ask her.

"Well, I can't today."

"That means you never will."

"Not *never*..."

"You know what I wish? I wish I was dead. Then I could see you whenever I wanted...even in the shower."

"God, Tommy," she said, "Settle down a little, will ya?"

It was that half-smiling, half-concerned look that seemed to characterize the way people saw me. Like there was something wrong with me and I should always be approached cautiously.

My only consolation for rejection was to browse through porn magazines at the Crown Books store by our house and ease my mind by fantasizing about what I couldn't do in reality. I started out going to read music magazines until I discovered that Hustler was equally accessible. Then I would crouch in a chair in a corner of the store pretending to read a rock and roll magazine while really scanning pictures of naked women and various sexual acts that I'd slipped between the covers of Hit Parader.

It wasn't long before Andy joined me one afternoon. When he saw what I was doing he laughed.

"Don't you know there's a better way to do it? You can read them in peace and not have to look around all the time like some guilty piece of shit."

He showed me how easily the magazines could be slipped down my pants. He told me that if I had a jacket on I could just slip the magazines inside that. I liked that idea better. I took to wearing a down jacket in every sort of weather after that, so I could easily swipe whatever I needed, wherever I was. This was not always comfortable or inconspicuous, but I did enjoy the reward of freely browsing porn in the privacy of my own bedroom.

Later that year Andy went to Sylmar Juvenile Hall. I missed him and because I wanted to be like him, I figured it was only a matter of time before I followed in his footsteps. My other buddy, Rich Andreas, also went to juvy after he was arrested for selling cross tops and pink hearts. I had first tried the pills with him earlier that year and now he was gone. Gone with him was the opportunity to enjoy that euphoric high I had experienced with my first use of speed. Also, despite a few repeated requests, I never did get that gun. Even my thoughts of suicide seemed like a failed and unrealized dream. While the thought of leaving this world was always a temptation, I resigned myself to finding other ways to self-destruct.

And then there was Gina.

I got along with everyone pretty well, in spite of the fact that I had so much unresolved pain. I had about a dozen guy friends, but we bonded mostly over weed and music. My overwhelming interest was in girls and there were a handful of them that I would hug every time I saw them. Even that brief contact meant a lot to me. Still, I had absolutely zero game to get past that superficial intimacy. I didn't even realize that I had a wall up that would hinder me in relationships for years to come.

The thought of being with any of these girls intimately was a comfort. I craved understanding and compassion. I wanted to be held and told that I was alright. I needed to be reassured that I was not the sick, dirty, disgusting fucker that I thought I was. Then, one morning at school, in walked the new girl. She was different than all the other girls and wore a lot of different colors. She carried herself with a foreign composure; Italian, French, or Spanish maybe. She looked exactly like Madonna at the time, whose look and style were breaking new ground. Beneath all of this, I recognized that she was shy and had something troubling her, too.

Her name was Gina and we had only one class together. It took a few months, but I finally got moved to a seat right next to her. I was always getting moved around in class—mostly for bad behavior. When I sat down, Gina looked at me and glanced as quickly away, embarrassed. It may have been a reaction to the teacher disciplining me or to the excitement I betrayed at getting to sit next to her. Either way, her reaction did not deter me.

Over the next few weeks, Gina and I became close. She told me about the difficulty she had with some of her teachers and I got angry for her, stuck up for her. She liked that I cared. I saw that deep down she was a good girl, just troubled. A few weeks later she didn't come to class and I learned that she had been expelled for telling her P.E.

teacher to fuck off. I couldn't imagine her doing that because all I saw was a shy, soft-spoken, and warm girl. I called her later that day and she admitted that the rumors were true.

With Andy and Rich gone, and now Gina, I wanted nothing more than to join them. I figured if I proved I was a tough kid I would get the respect of the girls and the street credit I coveted. I didn't realize it then, but I had already made the decision to live my life a certain way—to follow chaos and trouble. So often this is the only way kids know how to express their pain and confusion. Whether I craved negative attention or it was simply all I knew, I can't be sure.

One day I was in a ceramics class upstairs and I was ready when this Mexican kid Julian started talking shit to me. He was just messing around but I was past my tipping point and anything or anyone to set me off would have pushed me over the edge. It just happened to be him that day. In a heartbeat, I knew that I would fight Julian and I knew that I would have the advantage. I stood up and pushed him. He came at me and I grabbed his head and pushed him into the door. The door had a metal shelf jutting out and he struck his head square in the middle of it, crumpling to the ground. In another moment he was on his feet, stumbling toward me, but by then the teacher was separating us and a proctor had come flying through the door to haul me off to the principal's office.

I spent the rest of the day there, with a permanent scowl on my face. Now I was on my way to earning the reputation I was looking for. Everyone I saw that day deferred to me. My buddies were all praise: "I can't believe you beat up Julian, man," and, "Dude, that was legendary," were the comments they offered and each one bolstered me.

I was, at last, succeeding in something I had set out to do.

My mom showed up at the school and sat with me in the principal's offer as he delivered the verdict that I would be expelled.

"What does this mean for him? Can't he go to school?" My mom looked confused and more than a little ashamed.

"Well, he can't go to school here. There may be other options, other schools…"

When my dad found out about this later, I was in big trouble. But none of their preaching and none of their anger and disappointment had any bearing on me. I was, when it came down to it, angry that they didn't understand me. I was angry at their rules and their religion, because I believed in none of these things. These things were illusions and they had failed me. I would fail them, too. Eventually, I thought, I would try to make it to jail and try that on for size. I'd show them all what I thought of their fucking cult.

My parents had many long discussions behind closed doors after that incident and the result was that I started attending Patrick Henry Junior High School. I felt more alienated than ever in a new school. It was bigger, or at least felt bigger because it was new to me, and it was full of kids who neither knew nor respected me. It was easier for me to slink inside of myself and put the front on that I had shit going on and I wasn't about to waste my time in class or in the cafeteria talking about it to anybody. I warmed up to the few people I knew—the few people that "got me." But outside of that, I was on edge. I always felt that I would have to fight to prove or maintain my fragile identity, and I knew I could if I had to. But I have never been tough on the inside. I was always afraid of getting my feelings hurt or hurting someone else. And that was really the heart of the matter—everything I did was an attempt to protect myself and my deplorable vulnerability.

I soon found out that kids on the edge get handled a little more carefully. In my case, I went to a seminary class in the morning that was taught by Andy's mom. Even though she had a difficult relationship with Andy, she was a kind woman and was loving to me. She hugged me and told me I would be alright. It was exactly what I needed and it meant a lot to me. Years later, I told Andy this, but their relationship had always been a source of pain for him. I guess we are often harder on the ones we love.

As part of the bargain for attending seminary, I was given a note that permitted me to be released from school at 1:00 p.m. every day. It was easy enough to add another "1" and release myself at 11:00 each morning. Even though I had an apparently legitimate excuse to be out on the streets before noon, the cops didn't hesitate to question me frequently. My friends would often ditch school to hang out with me, but much of the time I was alone. When the end of the school year approached and the rest of the school began practicing for our commencement ceremony, I had no idea because I wasn't there.

Meanwhile, Gina's family had plans to send her to Ecuador to live with some extended family. She was bummed out and asked if I could make it over to see her. I hopped the 420 bus to Van Nuys, where she lived in an apartment with her mom. I was used to making trips to Sylmar during the day with Andy or one of my other friends and sometimes we would run into my Aunt Cheryl who was always strung out and looked to be prostituting herself on unprofitable corners. Other times I would be high on weed myself and would see someone who looked like my dad, setting off a fit of paranoia.

That day was different. That day I was on my own, going to see Gina. Past the bus stop, it was quite a hike and it was hot outside. I was trying not to sweat, but my nerves and excitement weren't making it easy. By the time I arrived at her run-down apartment building on Sepulveda and Lanark, I was a mess of anticipation. She smiled shyly when she saw me at the door.

"We have to go outside," she whispered.

I nodded and made my way down the stairs with her behind me. We found a shady spot under a tree on the far side of her building and sat together against a wall. She talked about how unfair it was to be sent away, to another country no less. I told her about getting kicked out of school. We talked about music and friends and how she hoped she might not be gone long. The sun started to dip in the sky and there we were, making out in the parking lot. I felt loved, supported, safe, and understood. It was everything I'd been craving, right there in my arms. I was intoxicated by nothing more than her eyes. I didn't know it was the last time I would see her.

A few days later, I heard that she had left. I called her at home and got no response. This was the fertilizer on my growing abandonment issues, and the pain tore at me. I was more alone than ever. A month later, I got a letter from Guayaquil, Ecuador, where she was staying with some aunts and uncles. In the letter, she told me all the things I wanted to hear. She told me how great she felt when she was kissing me, how sweet, loving, and good-looking I was—everything except that she was on her way back.

After all was said and done, I would wonder if it was really me she needed or just somebody. Is there ever really one special person we need, or is it just *love*? I didn't really know her, but I needed her. I didn't know the source of her pain and she didn't know mine, but through our mutual hurting, we understood each other.

After about a year and a half of mushy love letters and occasional long distance phone calls, the day of reckoning came. Her cousin answered the phone and greeted me in a snotty tone.

"She's out with a boy, you know."

I was crushed and cast down to the lowest of lows. I immediately penned a letter that read simply: *Gina, Fuck off! –Tommy*. I never spoke with her again. I tried months later, when the loneliness was hard to bear and I was desperate for a loving female. She didn't respond.

I was developing another awful defect: spite. When I was hurt, it was hard to focus on anything besides the pain and I would want nothing more than to hurt the perpetrator back. I could never turn the other cheek, because that would take an internal strength that I did not have. I thought it made me weak to let someone hurt me. I always had. And so I pretended that the small inflictions of pain— by Craig, the church, my parents, Gina—were nothing to me. I was a soldier in my armor: nothing could wound me. But in reality I'd built the armor around the pain, locking it all inside. The truth is, after thirty years I still have a cursive "G" tattooed on my left hand. I still love her, too. I love her in the way I love all the people who have come before, the people who have loved, the people who are hurting. We seem to be the strong ones, but we're not. There is a simple, vulnerable truth in each of us.

CHAPTER FOUR

1984-1986

My mom started to ask me when our commencement ceremony would be and I had nothing to tell her. I didn't know. I brushed her off and told her to stop bugging me. I wanted to live my own life. I didn't need her pestering me about some stupid graduation ceremony.

"Well, do you need to dress up for it? I can buy you a shirt."

"Mom, come on, get off my back! I don't even know if I'm going."

She stood in my doorway, torn for a moment between pushing the issue or letting me be. There are these moments of hesitation that we always think about later. What if I had let her buy me a shirt? What if she had insisted? She turned, after a moment, and walked away down the hall.

Between then and graduation, I spent more time standing outside of the school and smoking than I actually spent within the walls of Patrick Henry Junior High. When the day of commencement came, I got out of school early, as usual, and was loitering outside listening to Motley Crue on my Walkman and forging my goal to be full of attitude like Nikki Sixx. I saw the rest of the kids lining up for the ceremony. The parking lot was full of cars and parents gathered on the field behind the school in white plastic chairs that had been set out for the occasion. For a long moment I stood there watching and felt a twinge of regret. Then I lit another cigarette and turned the music up, listening to metal that cut straight to the heart of matters.

The first time I got arrested was for stealing a motorcycle from a kid around the block. I hid it good and when the police came around questioning us, I lied well. It was Jason across the street who ratted me out. They arrested me and booked me and then let me go when they got the kid's motorcycle back. After that I pretended to be mad at Jason. He'd always been a little smaller and a little weaker than me so it was easy enough to play the victim and get him all stirred up and feeling bad. After a while I let him off the hook. He was still my best source for good weed.

That summer I smoked crack for the first time. Some of my friends and I sat in a pristine, upscale kitchen with this Russian kid from school who showed us how to cook it up into a rock and smoke it. I took my first hit off of that glass pipe and fell backwards. My head was ringing like a bell. It was a crazy high but it didn't last long and left me wanting to catch it again. I'd done coke before and with that I could still function, but crack was all-consuming and, we soon found out, very expensive. It put me on a different planet and I wanted more.

Ken Jensen, who lived in my neighborhood and also went to Patrick Henry with me, was still the ringleader of the guys in the neighborhood and he was fortunate enough to have Jamie as a little brother. We were all glad to have

Jamie around, especially when we needed money for coke and he was the only one small enough to fit through the doggy doors of empty houses. We'd watch for people to go off to work in the morning and then Jamie would crawl inside of one house or another and take money or anything that we could turn into quick cash, like jewelry. We always joked that he was small enough to be a kid and if he got caught he could just say he was getting a lost ball from the backyard.

Running from the cops became a lot more dangerous, because now we had drugs, alcohol, and sometimes burglary on us. Back then LAPD was just as concerned with stopping kids from skipping school as they were stopping a bank robbery. I started running from them more often, and running hard. One day we were partying at an abandoned house and the cops started chasing us. Everyone scattered, but somehow they kept on me. I held out for a while and two helicopters started circling overhead. There were cop cars everywhere and a news crew that I didn't see but found out about later after they finally caught up to me trying to jump a fence in a nearby yard. My leg was grabbed by an officer and I kicked him in the face trying to free myself. I didn't know then that it was the police chief. He was just another enemy to me. They beat up on me pretty good and I felt the baton hitting my hip at full swing. There was a gun digging into the base of my back and a boot at the top, smashing my face into the sidewalk. I was slapped with at least ten counts of trespassing and resisting arrest. I didn't give a fuck about authority. I hated them and I was pretty sure they hated me.

That summer my sister's both went away to school in

Idaho. We'd always gotten along, but it seemed that I didn't understand them anymore and they didn't understand me. The only thing we had in common was an enjoyment of baking. My mom had taught all of us how to cook and bake and my favorite things to make were cookies and brownies. My sisters would come home and sit down to eat the warm treats, praising me for my skills in the kitchen. It drew us together, but at the same time there was that ever-present wedge. They had no inclination that my habits in the kitchen were motivated entirely by the fact that I almost always had the munchies. They saw, sometimes, that my eyes were bloodshot or that I wasn't talking like myself, but as with most things it was easier to ignore it than to face the possibilities.

"Why are your eyes always bloodshot, Tommy?" Tina asked once.

I shrugged my shoulders and Margie must have seen my discomfort. I couldn't seem to get the words out.

"Maybe he joined the swim team," Margie said sarcastically, coming to my defense.

Still, she looked at me askance and the awkwardness of those moments only made me want to stay away.

My parents subjected us, at that time, to one of the most horrific punishments imaginable to a group of siblings: the family road trip. We were all going to Idaho together to drop off Margie and Tina. Of course we bickered the entire way. I was upset that I had to be away from my friends and under the constant supervision of my parents. My sisters hated being trapped in a car with their younger siblings, and my brothers and I all wanted what the other had. There was no escape...it was exactly the type of situation I hated most.

When we arrived in Idaho though, and it came time to

say good-bye to my sisters, I broke down. I hadn't realized how much I would miss them. I hugged each of them and I knew they had a soft spot for me too. I'd always been the most loving kid in the family, despite my antics. I was always the one to feel things most deeply and to both give and receive affection most readily. Thinking about it now I wonder if this was not part of the source of my parent's frustration. On the surface, I was so close to being exactly what they wanted in a son.

With the girls gone, Tim was the oldest kid in the house and he reveled in this new role. He was harder on me than Tina and Margie ever were and he had no qualms about telling me exactly what he thought.

"Why do you hang around with those clowns?" he'd ask me often. Or, "What do you get out of that music?" "Why don't you just do what you're supposed to do instead of making trouble for yourself?"

I always thought it was easy for him to say. He was a big jock Mormon who good things came to and to whom good things would always come. He was constantly being rewarded and I was constantly getting into trouble and getting shit taken away. I was always told that the path I was on was a terrible one. I was always the butt of everyone's frustration. If they knew how bad it was for me, I think they would have done things differently. They would have wrapped their arms around me and said, "It's okay. It will be alright." And if I heard that, just once, I might have believed it, and it might have actually been true.

David and Dennis were in elementary school and they loved baseball as much as I had. I threw the ball around with them outside and pitted them against each other. I got to be the coach and the big guy with them that summer. They had the same athleticism that I had, but more of the determination. It was good to work with their ability and use it to teach them. It felt like I was doing something real. That time we spent together helped us bond and love each other as brothers. But by the end of summer I knew that it was time to leave those days behind. I told my dad I wouldn't be playing little league that year. I had better things to do.

In high school at James Monroe High, some friends and I ended up in jazz music class where I met Eckhart. Music class was supposed to be a good way to get free drum lessons, but it didn't quite pan out that way. The kids in that class all buckled down to learning their instrument, but learning the drums was a slow process that started with banging on some bells and clashing symbols here and there. I didn't have time for that.

One day I showed up to class late and drew the teacher's attention. He gave me a look and decided then and there that he would put the spotlight on the percussion section that day. He called us out and made us go through the music that he'd given us weeks ago. Of course I hadn't practiced so I just followed the lead of the other kids around me. All the while, my hatred of the teacher for putting me on the spot like that was welling up inside of me.

On top of that, this little prick named Jimmy was sitting at the drums in front of me and he was soaking up all the attention, banging away on those jazz drums like he'd been taking lessons all his life. He probably had. But his skill only highlighted my lack of it and my anger mounted. Couldn't they see that I was like Keith Moon, unorthodox and playing just for the thrill of it? Couldn't they see the talent inside of me? I hated Jimmy because I was jealous of his advantages. I hated the teacher for giving me a reason to feel embarrassed and conscious of my obvious inferiority. I had no tolerance for being embarrassed. The easiest reaction was always anger. Everyone else deserved the blame. *They* were the reason I suffered. The way I saw it, my only responsibility was to find a way to dull the pain. After band class, I did just that.

I checked out of band altogether after that and more often than not I found an excuse not to be there. My buddy Gary and I would ditch class and go to ABK Music Store around the corner and check out the guitars. He'd mess around with them while I listened to music on the store's headphones. The guy behind the counter knew we should have been in school but he got tired of asking us why we weren't there. He probably wrote us off. Most people did. The funny thing is, the more I got written off, the more I stopped caring.

When I first met Gary, I hadn't liked him either. He was a really good-looking surfer type and all the girls liked him. I got to know him on accident and when I did, I really liked him. He became my best friend for a couple years. It happened to me a lot that I would connect with people I didn't think I'd connect with. This is just further proof that even my best defenses were pretty thin. Gary and I were always riding around on skateboards, ditching school and looking for trouble. Our favorite thing to do was to hide behind a dumpster when the beer trucks were making their deliveries at the local grocery store. When the delivery guy disappeared inside with his first dolly-load of beer, Gary and I would grab a few cases off the truck and duck back behind the dumpster. If it wasn't delivery day, we'd swipe whipped cream canisters from inside the store and huff them out in the parking lot. It got us high for about five minutes and probably destroyed a few brain cells.

Before long, I was introduced to freebasing. Andy was back from juvy and we hung out more than ever. We had one quest: drugs and girls. The two went together and most of the time I thought of them as one and the same. Girls flocked to these guys and sometimes I would get lucky and hook up with a girl for a few hours. We'd smoke crack and the effects would last a while so I'd be hours late getting home. The last thing I wanted to do then was have a confrontation with my mom, but she was inevitably waiting up for me, by the phone.

"I called the Harding's. They said they didn't know where you were at."

"That's because I wasn't with Andy. Jesus, fuck! Why would you call them? I didn't tell you I was gonna be with Andy, so why would you embarrass me like that?"

"No, you *didn't* tell me where you were going to be. I had no other choice. I need to know where you're at when you don't come home!"

She was too stunned to comment on my language. Besides, it was the least of her concerns.

"Are you just *trying* to ruin my life? God, I hate you sometimes!"

I went to my room and slammed the door. I did hate her. I hated her guts for a long time. Every phone call she made was just another humiliation to get over; another nail in the coffin that would bury my image. In my mind, I had every right to lead the life I wanted to lead. I didn't owe her any explanations. I had built myself an image that left no room for a meddling mother. Sometimes a friend would say, "Hey, your mom called last night wanting to know where you were," and this was always said with a questioning look and I couldn't tell if it was the look that meant, "Man, why is your mom fucking crazy?" or the one that meant, "Here I thought you were a bad ass and you're really just a mama's boy." Either way, it was a judgment. Either way it was one more aspect of my life that I could not control. I know now that my mom was just trying to be responsible and take care of me, but she was ruining the image I'd built for myself—the one thing I had to cling to.

Eventually, in the 10th grade, I ran away from home. The first few nights I spent on the grass behind the grocery store. Then I went to my friend Eckhart's house. I told him that my folks had kicked me out of the house, because it sounded more pitiable. His parents agreed that I could stay with them for a while. It ended up being a few weeks that I was away. It felt like a long time. My parents didn't know Eckhart, so I felt like I was safe from their prying. Eckhart played guitar and our friends would come over and I'd sit there listening to them play guitar or bass. My own drums were sitting in my room at home. I had nothing to do but listen to these guys and tell them how good they played and we'd all talk about how great our band would be someday. MTV had come out not long before that so we watched a lot and dreamed a lot. Drugs and music went together almost as good as drugs and girls. And of course we talked about girls plenty.

"Tommy, you're pretty quiet over there. You still a virgin or something?"

The guys laughed the nervous laughter of teenage boys who've never been with a girl but want you to think they have. We were all full of false bravado.

"Of course I'm not."

"Well then, who've you fucked?"

If they knew the truth, I kept thinking. *If they only*

knew the truth...

"Gina."

Of course it wasn't true. But how would they ever find out? Gina was all the way in South America.

"Ohhh! Why didn't you ever say so?"

"I liked her a lot."

"Aw, Tommy's in love," they mocked, but it was believable. I wore my heart on my sleeve. And it was better than being mocked for something else. Those were the lies I told everyone else. I thought that if I could just make it true—if I could get with a girl—I would feel like less of a fraud. Everything would be better. These were the lies I told myself.

Being a runaway didn't get me any girls, but I felt like things were going okay. Then one night Eckhart's dad said, "Hey, Tommy, your mom called. She found our number somehow and just wanted to know that you're okay. What's that all about?" He and Eckhart's mom gave me that familiar sideways glance. That was what I was most afraid of, that these people would look at me and say, "What the fuck's wrong with you? You have a perfectly good family." Then they'd figure out that the problem was with me.

The following school year my attendance was so poor that my mom was called in and we met with a counselor.

"There are options for students like your son," he said, seeming to ignore the fact that I was also in the room. "Continuation school is often a good compromise. Many kids who struggle in the conventional school environment do better there because of the special attention that's given. There are incentives and they still get full credit towards graduation."

I could see, by the end of the meeting, that my mother had resigned herself to the idea. She didn't like it, but there was that faint aura of hope that clung about her. The counselor knew this. He dangled it in front of her like he probably had to dozens of parents. *Perhaps this will be the thing to set your child straight.*

I was all set to go to continuation school. I'd already had it in my sights. The campus was connected to that of James Monroe High and I was walking by one day, ditching classes, and saw a kid I knew standing outside of the little bungalow that housed the office of the continuation school. He had a garden hose in one hand, watering the flowers, and a cigarette in the other.

"Hey man, what are you doing?" I called.

"This is horticulture right here."

"Horti-what?"

"Horticulture. It's a class you can take here."

"You get credit for watering the fucking flowers?"

"Fuck yeah. We've got couches and shit inside, too, for naps."

"What about smoking? They let you smoke?"

He nodded, taking a long drag on the cigarette.

This was more my style, I thought. My friends and I smoked like chimneys before and after school, but we always had to be on the lookout for the undercover cops who patrolled the school. We had to ditch our weed whenever they came by. I could get used to this.

When I was enrolled in continuation school, I learned that I could either come for four hours a day every weekday, or for only one hour a day if I had a job. *You've got to be kidding me*, I thought. This was too good to be true. Now, I just needed a job.

Andy was working as a telemarketer for a solar energy company and he was the first person I hit up in my quest for a job.

"Yeah, it's pretty good," he said, "You sit in a room and you can smoke. You just sell stuff on the phone. And there's some pretty hot girls there, too."

That was all I needed to hear. Andy put in a good word for me and I was hired. I was making money and going to school for one hour each day. I loved it. Penny and Beverly were two of the girls we worked with and they were both smoking hot. Of course they were the girlfriends of the owners. I'd also started buying eightballs or quarter-ounces of coke and selling it off to my friends. I'd bring crack to work and even turned the girls on to it. The four of us would smoke it in the bathroom, but I never did have the confidence to get laid. One day, Andy said, "Hey, you know Tammy?" I didn't. "Well, she's been asking about you. You could get with her."

I hadn't noticed Tammy at work before, but I did then. She was decent looking and blond. She probably had confidence issues of her own because it wasn't long before she invited me over and gave me my first real sex. It was scary as hell but it felt great. The act only lasted about two minutes which was pretty sad, but she never complained and I didn't either. I was seventeen and a half and more relieved than anything to finally have a normal sexual encounter behind me. Still, it didn't erase the past or the pain. It didn't do any of the miraculous things I thought it would.

The job lasted about five months. Tammy and I never really amounted to anything. We were both locked too tight inside of ourselves to ever open each other up. Andy was like a big brother to me and he always had pretty hot girlfriends. Some of them he would even send my way when he had broken up or finished with them. Sex was a godsend and I was never happier than in those brief, earth-shattering moments of elation. But it was all a Band-Aid: the sex, the drugs, the music, and I was always hungry for more. Still, my miraculous salvation never came and I knew then that there was no such thing. Hope was an illusion for people like my parents to cling to. It was for the ignorant and church-fed believers, who did not see the truth, or live it, as I did.

One day, Andy and I were hanging out and smoking weed because we were both between paychecks and couldn't afford the good stuff.

"Did you hear about that fucker, Mathias?" he asked.

My insides went numb. I hadn't heard that name in years.

"No."

"Shit, he was a fucking child molester. He got caught up the road in Canyon Country. He was a fucking Boy Scout leader or a Big Brother or some shit. They said he molested like a dozen kids."

My heart was pounding. I took another hit. And another. It was a long time before I came out of the dark. When I did, it was like none of it had happened again.

There were only two other times when Andy mentioned him. One night he started laughing, saying, "Remember when that fucker Mathias had you doing jumping jacks? You took your pants off, didn't you? You did!" But he stopped there. I could see in his eyes that somewhere deep down he had made the association but did not want to explore it any further.

The other time, he mentioned Stephen Campbell.

"Yeah, he was probably one of Craig's victims. I remember he'd do everything with him. Small kid, not a lot going for him..."

Again, he seemed to reach a point where going further with these thoughts might mean a dangerous confrontation with reality.

"You know, that kid's dad wasn't really around," he said.

He waved it off like this explained everything away. He seemed to recognize that he was off track and slowly came around to a different subject. My face was burning. My insides quelled. I was thankful he let it go.

I hadn't run away from home since the first time, but that was mostly because I had more freedom now to come and go from home as I pleased. I was working, so I guess my parents let the reins out a little more, hoping it would take; hoping I would make something good of it. Sometimes I'd just stay out after work and crash at a friend's house. More often than not I made it to my one hour of class time at Albert Einstein Continuation School. I'd come home sometimes after being strung out for a few days and I'd walk in the door licking my wounds.

"You can't just come and go like a dog," my dad would say. "We can't have a son who just comes home when he's looking for the next meal."

But they always let me in. They always fed me. Maybe he was saying it more to convince himself that this was not what I had become.

It was a few months shy of the end of the school year when I was caught smoking crack in the bathroom at school. They didn't even kick me out. I had to meet with a counselor to revisit my education plan. I was on track to get

65

my GED by that summer. But by that time I'd realized that the only point to getting an education was to get a job and I already had one of those. I could make money and support myself. Just the week before, I'd been walking down the street to the bus stop and I'd seen a kid I knew a few years back. He was standing on a roof with his shirt off. He was tanned and tattooed and smoking a cigarette.

"What are you doing up there?"

"I'm working. I'm a roofer now. Dropped out of school last year."

That's the kind of thing girls like, I thought. Girls like jobs. They like a hard-working man. Girls don't like schoolboys who sell shit over the phone. Clearly I'd been going about this all wrong.

CHAPTER FIVE

2012

In October, the Boy Scouts sex abuse case broke wide open and their oft-publicized stance on gays was quickly overshadowed by a much larger scandal; one that included years of suppression of information in the form of "perversion files." The files, when brought to light, contained evidence that the Boy Scouts of America organization had been concealing reported abuse within their ranks since at least 1965. The paper trail they left implicated other organizations, like the Mormon Church, in the cover-up and showed a long history of not doing the right thing, simply to save face.

At about the same time, I received a response letter from the attorneys for the Church. It had been twenty-eight days since my letter was sent off and in that time I'd been doing my homework. I took it upon myself to gather as much information as possible about past cases, who had come forward with cases like mine, and the outcomes of these. It was then that I stumbled onto the case that was being handled by Portland attorney Kelly Clark. I watched as he won the release of the perversion files, which was a monumental accomplishment in trying to get these huge organizations to admit to secrecy regarding decades of sexual abuse.

I read and absorbed this information in earnest. Many a night, after the girls were in bed, Arlene had to pry me away from the computer. I would pull her close, having her sit down beside me while I detailed another story, another case, and we were encouraged by the trend toward uncovering this unsavory past. Arlene's excitement grew along with mine. I was dead focused on being a force for change, whether it was afforded through monetary compensation or the opportunity to help people. I saw the opportunity for my usefulness to many victims and survivors who would not or could not have a voice. Yet, knowing that the problem was so widespread and deeply entwined in our society was wearying, too. Each night I tucked the girls in and vowed to love them above all else.

I knew it was hard for Arlene at first. She, too, had a relationship with the Latter Day Saints, although hers was more favorable than mine. We were still attending church at our local ward because we didn't want to disrupt the girls' routines. They liked going to church. It had been a part of their lives and ours for the several years since Arlene had been called to the religion. I was a bit more circumspect. Now that I was making our family's involvement questionable, I was worried it wouldn't sit well with Arlene.

"I want to know that I'm doing the right thing for all of us, not just me," I said.

"Sometimes the best thing for one of us *is* the best thing for all of us. That's what family is."

The next day, after work and dinner and homework were done, I was back at the computer, delving into research. I learned that the Boy Scouts kept their documentation in some cheap filing cabinet in Irving, Texas. But that's just the way they are and this was no surprise. As soon as the perversion files were made public I was able to access them online. Up to that point I wasn't sure what had happened to Craig. I heard all those years ago about his arrest. Now I was able to see his file, which included a series of correspondence between the church, the Boy Scouts of America, and the Big Brothers organizations. They included newspaper articles covering his arrest. What I was able to see from this was that the church *had* likely reported Mathias's behavior, but still allowed him to get into a child-centric organization a few miles down the road where he could do it all again. These organizations had all been in on the cover-up together.

Of course the rest of the case files were protected in this case, so I had no way of knowing if the Church was found culpable in cases like Mathias's. I had no doubt that their fingers were in many of those pies. But they continued to be able to recover, cases were closed, and they hunkered back into their shroud of secrecy and holy alliance. The rest of us carried on with scars that never fade and nothing but a personal claim to the shelter of the Almighty. But after this I felt like all of the dominoes were falling in line; as if they'd been set up by a divine hand. The bigger picture was becoming visible. This only encouraged me that my own case was relevant.

Only now that I was prepared to come forward, I learned then that SB-131 was on the chopping block. Across California various groups were rallying to keep it alive. This was serious. SB-131 was my only window of opportunity and if it closed I would have no way of getting my case heard before a court. Essentially, passing the bill would allow more victims to take advantage of the extended statute of limitations and come forward with their cases. Vetoing it would effectively silence those who had already been silent for far too long. I decided to reach out to Governor Brown. In a letter, I wrote:

I survived aggravated rape as a thirteen year old boy in California, and I have been surviving ever since. I have endured many years of self-hatred, drug abuse, alcoholism, depression, and suicide attempts. Like most sex abuse victims, I did not deal with the root of these problems for at least two decades. For instance, in 2003, I entered yet another rehabilitation facility and could not even fathom dealing with the early abuse while I was still struggling with its residual effects, let alone seeking justice that was available within the "window" of that year. I now have over ten years of sobriety and am a positive and productive member of my community. I only recently started intense therapy for child sex abuse and am looking forward to making a big difference nationwide for statute reform. My point is that one cannot put a term on the time it takes for victims of abuse to recover and deal effectively with the perpetrators of these emotionally destructive crimes...

In the month before the response letter from the Church, I also contacted Dan Fasy. Dan was an attorney for Kosnoff Fasy in Seattle, Washington, a law firm notable for their involvement in significant child sex abuse cases against behemoth organizations like the Latter Day Saints and Boy Scouts of America. They sent a packet off in the mail for me to fill out and return. But you have to understand this about me: I am a personal guy. I like to meet people face-to-face. Something about the idea of putting my case on paper and mailing it off to an agency filled me with apprehension. There was nothing personal about any of it. Call me naïve, but I still thought there was some way to resolve the injustices of the world with raw human compassion.

And then the letter came. I had written my letter to the LDS church requesting that things be resolved without legal representation, but of course the response came from their attorneys, Kirton McConkie:

Dear Mr. Womeldorf:

We are in receipt of your September 5, 2012 letter to the Church and have been asked to discuss this with you and respond. Please contact me directly so we can discuss this matter. I look forward to speaking with you.

Sincerely,
Henry L. Scheffer

Well this is something, I thought. At least a prompt reply. But I felt outclassed. I talked with Paul and two other friends who were helping me--Kelly and Big Ernie--and the general feeling was that we were outmatched by the big attorneys. I knew I may not be able to go forward without representation.

Seeking to find a local attorney, Big Ernie referred me to Cameron and Moore, a local law firm in Scottsdale. I read up on them and found that they were primarily personal injury and criminal defense attorneys, but when I called them they were willing to meet with me and told me that one of their attorneys, Milton Moore, had some experience in handling a sex abuse case involving the Catholic diocese.

At home, Arlene and I were becoming more and more excited by the prospect of obtaining justice and being one more voice against the Church's secrets. Even Arlene was seeing that the problem was not with the religion, but with the institution. What I longed for was a committed attorney who would fight alongside us. Milton Moore was willing to take on my case, but he didn't demonstrate the kind of excitement I'd hoped for. I thought the evidence would speak for itself, but he didn't seem impressed by any of the facts I'd unearthed. It seemed that Arlene and I were the only ones spurred on by the idea that this case could have a monumental impact. My hopes were dashed a little by this.

"I don't think they understand what this means, or what I'm looking for."

"Well, what *are* you looking for?" Arlene asked.

"For acknowledgement. I want an apology and compensation. Not that giving me money would make a dent in the Church's pocketbook, but it would at least be tangible proof that what they did was wrong."

"And do you think this is the same thing the attorneys are looking for?"

"No. They want landmark cases, lots of money and prestige."

"Exactly. They're like insurance companies or casinos. They're all numbers. A corporation. So it's not monumental to them. None of these individual cases are. But this is the difference, isn't it—the difference between organizations and individuals?"

My first order of business was to call Moore, who asked me to send him a copy of the letter. I did one better and brought the actual specimen in person.

"I'll be drafting a response," he said, "and I'll have something in writing within a month. We'll outline your case for them and see how they wish to proceed. They may want to meet with you in person."

"I should hope so."

Moore looked at me and it was my cue to leave. He had other files awaiting his attention; other sheaves of papers that represented little more than an unrelenting workload. Arlene and I were both excited that things were finally happening now. They wanted to hear me. It was all I had hoped for.

Moore mailed a response letter dated November 14, 2012. It went one step further than my own letter had in outlining the details of my case, but I thought it did so without the personal touch and emotion that my own letter had conveyed. I was, after all, a real man with a real wound. Why must so much of life be spent in denying our own humanity and covering everything with formality? I'd spent decades numbing myself from reality. I damn well meant to embrace it now. So it was with some disappointment that I saw this most recent letter head on its way to the enormous clockwork system of cogs and wheels that was Kirton McConkie.

I tried to maintain a positive outlook. Throughout the process, I had been talking with family and friends and burning them out pretty quickly due to my unwavering enthusiasm. I'd been through so many years of therapy and confrontation with the past that I wanted to do nothing but talk about it. Still, I realized that for most people it wasn't something easily comprehended. Because of this, I rarely got the raw and brutally honest feedback I wanted. I heard about the Rape, Abuse, and Incest National Network which assists victims of these acts and I thought it would help to talk to someone who could relate to my attempts to deal with my past and reconcile my future by seeking justice.

73

The thing I'd learned is that there are infinite stages in the lives of survivors and that there is no point in trying to get through any of these alone. This was a new and significant stage in my own journey.

I contacted RAINN and they put me directly through to Empact, which is a suicide prevention and counseling center. I was connected to the Tempe, Arizona branch of the organization. I was impressed by how quickly I was able to reach live people who were there to support me. The organization is ready to serve every victim with the same urgency as a suicide hotline, patching them directly through to a local group. I had a long conversation with the folks at Empact during which they assessed me and decided to get me some one-on-one counseling. Almost immediately, I met with Conrad Brown and began this process. I never paid a nickel. RAINN was an amazing resource center and they supported everything. I was thankful for it and understood that *here* was an institution with class. There was no reminder of who'd helped me, no asking me to promote their cause, no hoops to jump through, no conditions. Just love. If I'd have had to pay for therapy, I probably wouldn't have done it because I would have put my family first when making the financial decision. These organizations must save a lot of lives this way. As for myself it never ceases to amaze me how much I have to learn. Sometimes we don't know how much we need help until we ask for it.

It wasn't until after the New Year that Moore received an informal offer from Kirton McConkie. He called me at home. The suggested settlement was a slap in the face.

"You should really consider the offer," he said.

I was not pleased. First of all, when I heard the numbers I was insulted. Secondly, I was appalled that

Milton found it acceptable. I sat there, listening to him and thinking of all that I had been warned about with regard to attorneys: that they're just looking for big money-making cases and if yours isn't it, don't expect them to be willing to go to bat for you. Now I realized my entire past, the pain, the struggle, the self-loathing, were nothing more than five digits on a page, and that was adequate for my attorney. For me, it was not.

"That's an insult. It's a pittance—an admission that they've done wrong but they can brush it under the table again by throwing me a bone. I can't take it."

"I think you have to separate yourself from emotion here. I think you need to stop and ask yourself what you really want to get out of this."

It was all I could do to restrain my temper. For a long moment I sat there and reined in all of the things I wanted to say. When I spoke, it was in a measured tone.

"I can't let them get away with it. If I take this, I'm letting them do it all over again. I'm letting them manipulate me. I *will* do this…I will get them to admit their fault and assign the proper value to it, but I will do it on *my* terms."

I hung up knowing it would be the end of our association. I didn't want to retain someone who wouldn't fight for me and who showed the same level of compassion as those puffed-up leaders of the church. Moore knew it, too, and didn't show any sign of emotion, true to his own advice. I was, once again, on my own.

The first thing I did was pen a letter back to Kirton McConkie telling them thanks but no thanks for their offer. I would give them one more chance to do the right thing and I offered to meet with them to reach a final agreement. Now that I had their attention, I wanted to handle this face to face. It was another month before their response came. They agreed to meet with me.

With my usual openness, I made no secret of any of these events and kept my parents and siblings apprised of what was happening. The week before, I had sent an e-mail to all of them:

Hi guys,

I want to let my whole family know of the latest challenge in my life. I want to assure you I have given you much thought, as this may be a very sensitive subject and I want to be as considerate and respectful as possible. My family has supported me through a very full life, to say the least!

I have been praying for a while now to be useful and courageous in great ways. Very recently, I showed up at work and the conference we were setting up from scratch was for Boy Scouts of America. The BSA and LDS church did a lot for my life that I do not regret. However, as you know, I have some serious issues I have dealt with for 29 years that relate to BSA and the LDS church. I have been moved to stand up for myself and help others, plain and simple.

I want you to know that I have mailed a personal and formal complaint to both parties. This does not declare my hatred of these organizations. It is simply a way for me to work out a problem that they and I both have and, again, to be useful in this life. I hope you can take this lightly. I am very open and unburdened by the events that are taking place as I feel very strongly in owning responsibility and doing the right thing.

Love, Tommy

I put this out there, knowing that not everyone would hold the same belief that I did that everything should be out in the open. I waited for the response. As always, I needed the love and validation of my family, but I also knew that I would continue on this path with or without them.

I spoke to Henry L. Scheffer and agreed to meet with him and another attorney. We set a date and I confirmed that I would not have an attorney with me. I was flying solo but whoever wanted to join me was welcome. I extended an invitation to Paul who had already helped me through so much of the process. My parents called and I told them about the meeting that would be taking place between myself, the church, and their attorney. But I hardly expected the reaction I got from my mom and dad.

CHAPTER SIX

1986 – 1990

It didn't happen gradually. I just stopped going to school. I took on a few more hours at the solar energy firm and then I hooked up with a guy from church named Jed who'd been in construction for a few years. He'd been around the block but he wasn't a fucking pedophile and he took me on. I started working with him and doing carpentry. We went to some real nice areas, in Beverly Hills and Malibu and places like that.

I started doing a lot of coke then. Freebasing was the drug of choice and it worked out really good because it was highly addicting and there were a couple streets a few blocks away from home—Columbus, Orion, and Langdon—that were dedicated to selling crack. I saw some horrific stuff happen down there in the time I frequented it. I saw a dealer shoot and kill a cop one night and then another cop shot and killed the dealer. Being strung out on that shit was nothing nice either.

The other problem was that I mostly still lived at home but my time there was becoming less and less. I spent more time crashing on other people's couches and my parents accepted it for the most part because I told them I had to be near wherever I was working. I got myself a street bike and used that to get around. It gave me a new sense of freedom and made it easier to be wherever I wanted and more convenient to get high. I can only assume now that my parents hoped I would develop a sense of responsibility with my new freedom, but this was not to be. And then there was Marilyn.

I'd known her for a couple of years as Andy's girlfriend. She was a short, Italian girl with tanned skin and these exotic green eyes. She and Andy tried to fix me up with friends of hers a couple of times and once or twice it even lasted more than a few weeks. For a short time, Andy and I rented an apartment above a tuxedo shop that his Grandma owned. Other girls came and went from our apartment, mostly for me, but Marilyn was a constant. I saw her a lot more often back then, but now I was broke and back home with my parents again. I was lonely and screwed up. Marilyn and I decided to meet to go Christmas shopping and she offered to pick me up in her car. She'd driven nice cars in all the time I'd known her. At that time she was driving a black convertible VW Rabbit, which was a big deal in the 80's.

After shopping we went to her mom's house where Marilyn lived, south of Ventura Boulevard. Her mom was an actress and I'd seen her on TV in years past and had a little crush on her at the time. But that was nothing new. I had always been preoccupied with fantasies of girls or women who might wash clean the memory of that sick fuck who'd stolen my only innocence. That night it was clear to both Marilyn and I where the night was going as soon as we started drinking. My desire for her was all-consuming. I was used to that—being carried away on the tide of distraction, whatever the distraction might be. If it was a girl, all the better. If I was lost in something it meant that I didn't have to be responsible for watching the signs and the markers. I didn't have to take the blame or feel the guilt of where I'd been and what I'd done. I determined to lose myself in her.

I was so drunk that night it didn't happen. She laughed and put me to bed. The next night was a different story. I'd never been able to connect with a girl like I connected with Marilyn. The sex was great and with her I was able to relax and exalt in the fact that she accepted me and that I was not repulsive to her. She didn't know me, of course, but I'd worshipped the ideal sexual act for so long that I interpreted it as a sort of revelation of the soul when it finally happened. It was the only time, I thought, when two people are really laid bare and open for interpretation. To think that a girl like Marilyn would see me that way and not find me wanting was a fix like no other. I saw that I could please her in so many different ways, and I didn't know it then but I began to reconstruct my image of myself because of this.

I basically moved into Marilyn's mom's house right away. Her mom wasn't too keen on me and that wounded me a little because I wasn't used to being rejected. People generally liked me. But she clearly had a different set of criteria. I wasn't showing the type of promise or potential that she wanted for her daughter. Well, so be it. I wasn't about to let it stop me.

Meanwhile, Andy caught wind of what was going on and he wanted to kill me. In my complete absorption in sex and belonging, I had failed to analyze this other aspect of the situation: that I was sleeping with my best friend's girl. All I saw then was that I had hostility on several fronts. I drank like a fish to cover the feelings associated with this.

That meant I didn't have to spend too much time looking closely at why I was such an object of disapproval. I tried to twist the situation in my mind and justify it as much as I could, but no matter how much I tried I couldn't be angry enough at Andy to fight him. So I avoided him instead.

Marilyn and I spent a month in honeymoon love, slithering and sneaking away. And then she started acting on her female agenda. I don't know if it's all girls or just the girls I had known up to then, but I had the impression that they all looked at a guy and thought, "This guy would be perfect if I could change..." and then the list began. I started to sense the conditions on Marilyn's love. As a guy—especially one whose self-esteem was as fragile as mine—this was hard to come to grips with.

Nonetheless, Marilyn got me to my first recovery meeting. It was on Comercio Way, in Woodland Hills. I was nineteen-years-old and the next youngest person in that room had to be pushing forty. They were mostly grandparents! I went along with the gag, all the while maintaining my internal dialogue that was bent on rejecting the whole thing. Sex was the carrot dangling in front of me and I would go along with most anything if it would keep getting me laid. The longest I went without drinking then was thirty-nine days. Then I slipped up for a week. The next time it was twenty days, followed by another slip-up. Still, Marilyn cared about me and the caring made a difference. My motorcycle got impounded and she drove me to work. I always had tickets and warrants for not showing up to court and she pushed for me to pay them off. She tried to take me in a different direction. After a year or so I got my act together. I bought a new truck. I moved out and we were fighting often then. In my twisted way I felt like I didn't really need her anymore now that things were going well for me.

Right around my twentieth birthday I got smashed at a party that may or may not have been my own. As drunk as I was, I offered to give a girl a ride home. We parked on the side of the road and I ended up kissing her and fingering her. I wanted to fuck her so bad, but I was paralyzed by guilt even through the haze of alcohol. I wouldn't have done it to be hurtful to Marilyn, but of course that's how it would be interpreted.

I said that I reconstructed my self-image because of Marilyn. It was not necessarily a good thing. I felt like if I was good for her then surely I was God's gift to girls and they just didn't know it. How long had I lived with this innate sexual prowess within me? Wasn't I doing an injustice to myself to spend it all in one place? I began to wonder. But really, it went deeper than that. I had found something to define myself by. I'd failed at everything I'd defined myself by prior to this. I was (obviously, I thought) a failed man at the core. I was a failed musician, a failed son, a failed student, a failed Boy Scout, a failure to God. What I succeeded at was being a drop-out, a druggie, a bad boy, and now a sexual virtuoso. I set the bar low because I knew I could attain that. And when I did, it felt *good*. I wanted more.

So I walked away from Marilyn. She didn't know why. She didn't know about the little floozy's pants I got into in the car. She didn't know about the guilt that reminded me of how much I hated myself and made me resent Marilyn by extension. I told myself I was being better than Andy who cheated on her behind her back. I told myself I was saving her from that humiliation by taking the high road. But really I was punishing myself by getting lost again.

There were a series of women after that. I picked up where I left off. Actually, it was even worse now that I actually knew how to satisfy a girl. I was less discriminate, more bent on proving something. I grabbed a thirty-nine year old in Hollywood who looked like Julia Roberts. She couldn't get enough of me which only perpetuated my idea that sex was what I was made for. A porn star I met at a twelve-step meeting brought me back to her apartment and fucked my brains out. I picked up another woman—thirty-five—from a 7-11 and was screwing her within two hours. I slept over at her apartment that night in Sherman Oaks. I met another girl at the Winnetka Drive-In while I was there with some pals. I was banging her within fifteen minutes of meeting her. We were in my friend's car and they were outside watching and pounding on the windows. I felt like I was well on my way to living the lifestyle of a sleazy rock star I'd always dreamed about.

All of this gave me some validation then, some reason for being. But even these ruthless brushes with complete abandon were not without their deeper connections. There is, among people, a tendency toward commiseration and so we get too close to the thorns when we are seeking beauty. No one escapes a walk through the garden without some scars. It was 1990 and I met this girl while driving on the freeway. We pulled over and she gave me her number. She was from Massachusetts and she was older—thirty-five. Her name was Christine. Older women were like a trophy for me and right away I was crazy about her. And that's the thing: I can recognize now that it was never just about sex. I've always loved people. I've always been driven to connect with them. I just didn't know how to do it in a way that did not involve sacrifice.

Christine was divorced and had a daughter who was

one-and-a-half so I had to go over to her house only when her daughter was asleep. A couple of times the little girl was still awake and I had to play with her and that was too much for me then. Kids are too truthful, like looking in a mirror. Christine said her ex-husband was abusive. His name was Frank and after a while I came to meet him, too. I saw Christine maybe once a week and a few times Frank was coming or going with their daughter. I was always on edge when he was over there, afraid that they were going to fight and I'd have to do something.

Then Christine asked me to help her move and told me that Frank was going to be there too. We showed up and it was awkward for a couple of minutes. Then we started small talk: *Oh, you need help with the couch there. Here, let me get that.* And then I saw Frank's daughter interact with him and I melted. I knew he was a crack head and a drinker too, but I just saw this guy who was like me but he was a father and somehow it touched me to my core. By the end of the day I loved the guy and just wanted to hug him and see him succeed.

A week later Christine told me Frank had hung himself on a street sign or something. I was stunned. I thought of that little girl who loved him. I thought about Frank's face when he looked at her: like he couldn't quite believe she was real. And I mourned for him. I really connected with him for a short time there. Two weeks later, I learned that the front-man of Mother Love Bone and another of my idols, Andrew Wood, was dead of an overdose. I had lived life on the fringes and worshipped these idols who represented all that I wanted to be. This all happened around the same time and even though they were separate incidents, I felt a connection with these people who had died so tragically. We're all so parallel, it seemed. They made the ultimate sacrifice and as I experienced what it felt like to mourn for them I thought that if I could inspire that feeling in others it might give some value to my life. You see, there's a thin veil between what is and what should be; between right and wrong. The lines for me had been blurred long ago.

Between long periods of heavy binging on alcohol and cocaine, I would go to recovery meetings. Sometimes because the court mandated it and sometimes out of loneliness. I was pretty aware of my condition and my hopelessness. I knew that these things defined me: I was an alcoholic, a drug addict, and possibly an awful, filthy, sexually twisted man.

In September of 1990, things started to derail. I'd tried to get back with Marilyn a few times when there was no one else, but it never worked. The house I had in Chatsworth was a rental and I had promised my landlord I'd fix it up in exchange for lower rent. Between changing jobs several times and spending all my money on binges, I found no time to hold up my end of that bargain. I turned my truck in for voluntary repossession after months of dodging the bank and the men they sent to collect the vehicle. I finally turned myself in for several unpaid warrants against me and did a four-week stint in jail. Meanwhile, I lost the job I was currently on and knew that it was a matter of time before I was evicted from the house as well. When I got out of jail I spent what little money I had left on crack and gallons of vodka, but these were just a Band-Aid to get me through the last days before the inevitable end. I began to think that those days were an obvious end to any prosperity I had enjoyed, and a likely end to my life itself.

I had no reason to live. I cried for days, holed up in

that house as the pain of loss and loneliness seeped into my bones. My Rottweiler, Sam, cried with me, more so because I couldn't afford to feed him than out of any real commiseration. I scoured the house for the sharpest, rustiest razor blade I could find. Satisfied, I went to the bathroom and sliced away at the insides of my elbows and my wrists. The blood started to flow, but I didn't stop until my body gave out.

CHAPTER SEVEN

1990 – 1994

I woke up without knowing how much time had passed. Coming out of that calm black nothingness was heart-breaking. I was propped up against the wall in the bathroom in a pool of my own blood. Sam the dog was licking my open wounds and I looked down to see that the blood there had dried. I had to look away, disgusted. Even more so, I was weak. It took me a long time to crawl to the phone. I saw that eight hours had passed since I took the razor blade in my hand. I pulled the phone down to the floor by its cord and called Marilyn. She was the one who I wanted to share my misdirected pain. In my distorted, selfish world, Marilyn was the one who had caused it. I had always felt like a dirty, used-up piece of shit when I was with her. I always felt that she would be looking for a better guy and failed to realize that she had only wanted to help me because she saw my potential, not because she wanted someone different. Still, I didn't know that my own insecurities fueled these thoughts.

She got to my house and called 9-1-1 and my mom, who met us at the hospital. They put over 120 stitches in my arms and the doctors told me later that they couldn't see how I didn't hit a main artery. My heavy slicing had only narrowly missed. To me, this only meant I was an even bigger failure. It was now documented and there were witnesses to prove it. To make matters worse, I thought I would never be able to use my arms again. Seeing that I did everything with my arms and hands: construction, drumming, holding women, riding motorcycles, fighting, it was only fitting that I should lose this too. I didn't move much for a week or so, but gradually I got the use of my arms back. Now I was even more depressed, if such a thing is possible. As for the rest of the people in my life, I think they could only handle so much. My parents were uneasy, on eggshells, and seeing their reaction made me even more loose and distant. I understand now that they didn't really know what to do. They made these feeble attempts at fixing me but they weren't able to acknowledge the worst of it. Even then, I don't know if I was ready to acknowledge it myself.

Back at home, and fresh off of an attempted suicide, my prison was getting cold. It was November and the gas had been shut off months ago and there was no hot water or electricity for the appliances. I started using only the family room and the bloody bathroom, bundling myself in blankets at night—some still bloody because I couldn't use the washer and dryer. I took ice cold showers when I had to and still barely moved my arms for fear of popping the stitches. How could I blame anyone for not wanting to descend into my private hell?

I knew I had to find work and talked to Jake who had been a friend of mine for a long time. He and Andy both had their own businesses then doing hardwood floors in Hollywood Hills and Beverly Hills. Andy and Jake were totally different people. Andy would drink and smoke but that was about it. Even that he wouldn't do much anymore. He was never big into drugs once he got out of high school. He tried just about everything but he wouldn't spend money on it. Jake made even more money than Andy but he would blow right through it on booze and drugs. He went through an entire inheritance, smoking crack and buying things. I liked hanging out with him because he liked to party and didn't hold back. Andy would only party if I was buying. I didn't hang out with him much anymore for that reason alone. But he was always there for me. After he got over what I'd done with Marilyn, he and Rich were among the few who came to check on me when everyone else was leery and distant.

Jake gave me a job working with him and I bought an old 1971, pea green station wagon for $250. It had faded wood paneling and was longer than shit. It looked like an ocean-liner. Even though I started to get back on my feet, people treated me differently. It was like they were afraid I was going to try to kill myself again at any moment. Jake was a good guy though, and he gave me the benefit of the doubt. He had a guy working with him named Todd Barley, who was about fifteen years older than me. He was from right outside of Boston.

It wasn't long before I started making decent regular money and got to drinking again. Todd lived in a guest house that he called "the cabin" because it sat on two acres of land and had some woods behind it. Jake started inviting me over there by saying, "There's always plenty of Rolling Rock beer at the cabin." That was a good enough endorsement for me! I moved out of my rental just as the sheriff arrived to give me the boot and moved in with Todd. I worked, did laundry, and spent too much time with him. We listened to Howard Stern in the mornings as we laid there in the one big room opposite the kitchen. I remember the morning in 1992 when we heard on the radio that Sam Kinison had died in a car wreck. They did a lot of great tributes and stories about him. He was quickly becoming one of my favorite idols again, filling me with that old taste of the forbidden glory that comes with a tragic end. He'd done lots of coke and drinking during his life which happened to be what I was doing more of, once again.

Enough was never enough for me. I had to go overboard. I had to obliterate my mind and kill the pain. This, I saw, was what differentiated me from others of my friends who were not so obsessed. One Sunday morning, after a two or three-day bender with Todd and his friend, Bobby, we drove up to Santa Barbara. We hit a bar or two for drinks and of course went in search of cocaine. The rest was sort of a fog until the following Sunday morning when the neighbor or someone pulled me up out of it, yelling at me about the dog.

Passing out was my body's only answer to the onslaught of drugs and it was often the only period of rest I had. I dragged myself outside to see what the fuss was about. There I saw Sam crouched in the middle of the yard with a dead bird. He was growling and backing everyone off him so I went toward him to set him straight. As I approached he showed me his teeth and tested me. I was about to give up, mostly because I was still weak and shaky and didn't need the bother. Then I turned around and whipped him off the bird and became the boss again.

A couple months later, Todd moved back to Massachusetts and left me the cabin and most of the furniture. Left on my own again, the drugs and alcohol got heavier and more frequent. My friend Mardi moved into a trailer next door and I loved hanging out with him but we were both addicts and he would always hold out on me.

One night I was hanging out with Robbie, who I'd known for years. We'd all grown up in the same neighborhood and he was a few years older than Andy. Robbie and his buddies used to beat up on Andy when they were kids. That's how Andy got tough and later on he could beat them up and hold his own. Robbie was a scrawny, buck-toothed kid. He was a derelict, even as an adult. He'd done stints in juvy and prison over the years and then he'd pop up with a stolen car or money and I'd end up hanging out with him. That night we got together and started doing coke.

We set out on our bikes to get more at 3 a.m. and then again at 5:00 the next morning. We were out of money and out of options. It was another three or four hours until any of the check cashing places on Reseda and Roscoe opened up. In those few hours, Robbie came up with the bright idea to write out one of his dad's checks. When the place opened, I went in to cash it. I thought it was taking a long time for the teller to get me my money, but my senses were pretty distorted. I tried to calm down. I'd been up all night smoking and drinking and I was desperate for more. Then, out of the corner of my right eye I saw a dark figure crouching down and going behind me along the glass front of the building. Was I hallucinating? I saw another then, right behind me and more clearly. Two LAPD officers came charging through the front door and tackled me. What a great Saturday morning it was turning out to be.

As the cops dragged me from the building, I knew that Robbie was across the street watching. While I was in the cop car Robbie's dad showed up and he was not looking too happy. So, off to jail I went. I was handcuffed in the backseat, trying to figure out how to get the dirty crack pipe out of my jacket and get rid of it. I wished then that I had quit the coke smoking binge and just drunk myself to sleep the night before, but that wasn't the deal. My addiction was an 800-pound gorilla that could sit anywhere it wanted to. I was never done with the drugs until the drugs were finished with me.

We got to the police station and they walked me in. My window of opportunity was closing to get rid of the pipe and I began to realize that I wouldn't have a chance. As suspected, they found it when they were booking me and I said nothing.

"You'll be looking at more time for this," the cop said, holding it up for me to see as if I wasn't already familiar with all the burnt coke residue in it.

A few hours later I was brought into a room to hear the charges I was facing. Possession was not one of them and I felt that it was just one more instance of God holding back. The forgery alone, however, was enough to put me in prison for one to three years. I knew this was serious. I reached out for help in the only place I thought I would find it. I called my parents.

When my mom answered the phone I tried to act like everything was normal. Then I told her I was facing prison time and tried to justify everything as it was my habit to do. My mom listened and then she said, "Hold on just a minute, Tommy." It was kind of quiet and she covered up the phone. I knew she was talking to my dad. After a long while she got back on the line and said, "We really can't do anything, Tommy. We just can't help you this time." It shocked me, but it shouldn't have. They had clearly thought about it. They knew what they were going to do when that day came and they did it. It must have been hard for them, but even I knew that it was the healthiest move they could have made.

I was sitting in the cell, totally dejected and facing prison. I kept thinking about the harm I was going to give Robbie when I got out. I took a nap and read some of the days-old newspapers and slept some more. Jail at least allowed me to rest and recover from the self-inflicted damage I was doing. I was sitting and staring at the wall when in walked Robbie. I thought I was dreaming or hallucinating. My mind immediately jumped to how I could pay him back for landing me in there and he must have seen it on my face because he was goofy and laughing like it was all normal to him.

"You're free to go," he said, "I took the blame for everything."

I didn't know what to believe and he just kept laughing over how angry I looked. There he was, facing prison time with a smile while I was ready to head back out onto Van Nuys and Victory Boulevard. I don't know which of us had it better. Either way, I found my way back to the cabin and got on the phone to see what kind of trouble I could stir up.

Life continued as normal as normal was for me. I got pulled over again that summer of 1992. It was the third of July and Andy and I had driven to Lake Pyramid, next to Castaic Lake, for the Fourth of July holiday to drink and boat and waterski with some buddies. When I heard the sirens and saw the lights flashing in the rearview, I dropped a big vial of coke on the seat. When the cop was talking to me I was looking down at the coke and laughing inside because he wasn't seeing it. If only he looked down, I would have been in a world of hurt.

To cause a distraction, I bent to fish for my license and

registration, which of course I didn't have. The truck had Iowa plates and the registration was long expired.

"I'm sorry. Everything is in such disarray," I said, knowing that would make Andy bust a gut.

His laughter had the opposite effect of lightening the mood and the cop got angry. It was just the distraction I needed though and it saved me that day from getting busted for coke as well as for driving an unregistered vehicle.

Andy didn't really do drugs so I always downplayed my use with him. Even after the fiasco with Marilyn, he found it in his heart to forgive me and just love me for who and what I was, without knowing the full extent of that. I was hauled off to Valencia police station and back to jail. I did about three weeks for the DUI and registration violation. I told Andy about the coke later and he laughed a little but mostly blew it off, which made it easier for me to do the same.

A few months later I went to Yuma, Arizona with another friend of mine named Dan. We went to visit a Marine buddy of his who had a family and plenty of beer. We must have drank thirty or forty beers each, every day of that Thanksgiving weekend. And on the last night we went to a bar and decided it would be more fun if we were packing heat. Dan and I were amazed that it was actually legal to carry guns in Arizona (except to courthouses and bars), so of course we gave in to temptation and bent the rules for that occasion.

On one of my countless trips to the bathroom to piss out a massive volume of beer, I started to ask everyone I passed, loudly, "Who has the coke?"

The bar was pretty well-stocked with Marines and they were cool with alcohol and guns, but drugs weren't really their thing. Still, I managed to track down a guy who had some coke and he put a small amount out for us. It didn't really affect me, just teased me and I thanked him but couldn't resist throwing in, "You should try actually getting high from it sometime!"

I was lucky I made it out of there intact. The trip ended and Dan told me he wanted to give me his old Toyota Celica, since I was now without a truck and he was in the market for a new one. It was one of the nicest things anyone was doing for me then and more than I deserved. I went along with it even though the car had Ohio plates and meant I'd probably be stopped again for non-registration. But that was a problem for another day.

The cabin continued to be an alcohol and drug haven. The interesting thing is that we were all addicts but we really never cheated each other. There was a good amount of love for all the sickness.

1992 was a fast year and before I knew it that summer was over and fall was fading to winter. The week before Christmas, my brother-in-law John, who was Margie's husband, helped me move out of the cabin in a hurry to avoid Victor, the Hungarian landlord, and the debts he intended to collect on. My friend Josh and I stayed with Margie and John for a few days and then we loaded up Josh's white '92 IROC and headed out for Monroe, Louisiana with the idea of staying with his mom for a while and getting clean.

Josh's mom, Tracy, had fled Los Angeles ten years earlier and I always suspected that she may have been under the protection of the witness relocation program. She'd been a junkie and a pill-head through the '70's, running with musicians and criminals. It was a long ride to Louisiana, but we had a couple days' worth of pot and speed to sustain us. Even with stretching it out we ran out too soon and stopped in Tucson, Arizona where we stayed up all night with some college kids who had drugs.

The next night we slept in the car in El Paso, Texas, because we heard that cars disappeared fast there since it was so close to the Mexican border. Josh was pretty attached to his third gen Camaro. The next night we got a room and some sleep in Fort Worth and the following day saw us all the way to Monroe.

By some stretch of generosity and good faith, my dad saw fit to give me a Texaco card before we left on that trip. It was a cruel twist of fate that the Texaco up the street from Tracy's house was tied up with a Cracker Barrel Store. The first person we met in Monroe was Tanya who was a cashier there and she introduced us to the MD 20/20, which was a cheap but toxic wine drink. Of course we started swimming in it and by the time the first month was up and the credit card bill was sent home, my dad was irate. He somehow convinced me to send the card back.

Tanya was a single mom and lived with her parents. That February they had Josh and I over for the Super Bowl and it was awkward and comical by turns. Once the jig was up and we lost our outside funding for frequent trips to the store, though, we didn't see Tanya much anymore.

Around that time I bought a magazine that was all about the Seattle music scene. They had a piece in the magazine about Mother Love Bone and Andrew Wood. The rock and roll lifestyle was everything I dreamed of having for myself and I actually believed then that I could put a whole concept and band together and go back to take Los Angeles by storm. It just shows how far from reality I had strayed.

The rest of the year passed with us hanging out with Josh's step-dad, Myron, who was the town shyster and played organ and keyboard with some of the local bands. Josh and I would help him haul his gear from his old Cadillac into the cheap bars where he played. He bought us drinks for being his roadies.

After a year, Margie told me that she and John wanted to come out to visit us for Mardi Gras. I wasn't thrilled about having the older married couple there. As a resource they were welcome, but other than that I just saw their visit as an imposition. They came out and Josh and I met them in New Orleans. We partied for two weeks straight and Josh and I were drunk one night when the obsession for crack overtook us. We ended up a few blocks out of bounds—in the projects. We bought some bad stuff and it took me on the worst trip I'd ever been on. I was angry and yelling racial slurs, challenging strangers on the street and even Josh. It was pretty ugly.

After that, Margie started to press her agenda and asked me to come back with her and John to California. I didn't know why my family always did this. Their attempts to shelter me were banal and I always felt it was just another sign of how little they understood me. I belonged out there, roaming the earth. Still, I was only occasionally working in Louisiana and the rest of the time I was mooching off of Tracy and Josh. I would help them and Tracy didn't mind it, but I didn't like living off of anyone like that. So after a while I gave up trying to fight it and I agreed to go back to California with Margie and John.

I lived with my sister and her husband for a while and they got divorced nine months later. John was a screwed up guy who had similar demons as me and Margie had been with him for a long time before she realized their relationship was going nowhere. Not that I helped much, other than to speed things along. I've always been there to help people go down the tubes farther and faster. I'd gotten used to the idea that chaos followed me around like a dingy shadow, but again, I didn't see it as something I had any control over. I couldn't understand why people were so uptight and I thought everyone should live and be their authentic selves. That was the way I was living my life and it was working for me, or so I thought. But who was I to pass judgment? I didn't even know myself. What I did know was that my beautiful sister deserved better.

During that summer of '93 I reconnected with my cousin Wyatt and his friend Jordan Paxson. They were doing a lot of meth and drinking so I fit right in. We based our operations out of Wyatt's bedroom at my Aunt Jean and Uncle Jim's house in Northridge. Those were the days of all-nighters and two, three, and four-day benders. We would stay up and play cards then clean carpets during the day and go to bars until it was time to do it all over again. The people I met then were a blur and that's sad to me because people have always been the most important thing. We'd crash at their houses and never leave a trace of ourselves in the lives of others. It was a bizarre time.

Then, on a four-day bender in August, we went to see one of Wyatt's best friends, Luca Adrian, who was a singer. He was staying at his bandmate Rocky's classy house in Woodland Hills. Rocky's parents were out of town so he had the place to himself and it was soon crawling with the likes of us. Wyatt's girlfriend Kristy was with us and we were touring the place. We stopped in the hallway near Rocky's bedroom and saw a door standing open. Inside was an elegant bathroom with this huge tub that was framed in mosaic tiles. Wyatt let out a whistle and Kristy laid herself out in the tub talking about how great a life it would be to take baths in a place like that.

We left that night because Kristy had to get home, but Luca stayed there with Rocky. The next day we heard that Luca got a gun out of the master bedroom closet the night before and blew his head off in that same bathtub. There was heroin involved, so we never knew if he overdosed and Rocky shot him, or if he just decided to put an end to the hard times.

When Margie and John were going through their divorce I had nowhere to stay so I crashed at my parent's house when I wasn't at Wyatt's place. Suddenly, at 4:00 in the morning on January 17, 1994 I was jolted awake. The entire foundation of the house was shaking. I was sleeping on the floor in the spare bedroom after another bender when the Northridge earthquake hit. I scrambled out of the crowded room as things started to fall from the shelves and the bed bounced toward the window. If that was instinctual, then so was what happened next. I fell to my knees in the hallway. Not because I tripped but because I was ready to accept the house falling in around me. I waited there for the walls to crumble and bury me. At least the roller-coaster ride of life would be over.

The shaking lasted for a couple long minutes and when it was over I stood up and was almost sorry that I was able to do so. The house did not collapse, and the drama of life continued. A few weeks later, Theresa came into our lives.

CHAPTER EIGHT

1994 – 1998

Theresa was the long-time girlfriend of Luca Adrian, who ended up dead in Rocky's bathtub. She was traumatized by this and in her confusion she reached out to a big, black drug-dealing pimp named G-Rollin', who was also known for some other nefarious dealings. Theresa believed that Rocky was responsible for Luca's death and she meant to seek retribution. Her dad was a retired LAPD officer and he told her that there would be no money spent on investigating the case. Luca's death was a suicide on the books and that's how it would remain. Theresa was small, but she was power-hungry and smart. But her plan on that occasion backfired. She was gang-raped by the pimp and two of his friends. This all happened a couple of weeks before I met her.

She came in like a tornado. According to Wyatt she'd always been that way, but now she had some extra baggage in the way of panic attacks and paranoid delusions. I was, of course, intrigued by her. Wyatt and Jordan both laughed at me.

"No way, man. She's nothing but trouble."

What I saw was a girl who acted on her impulses and I

liked that. The first time I met her she launched into a rant about the IRS and her plan to shut them down. Despite their warnings, Jordan and Wyatt both had girlfriends so that meant Theresa and I had plenty of occasions to talk.

"I'll tell you what that mother-fucker did," she said, "he said he'd do what I asked in return for a favor. He had me show up and date this old man and do whatever he wanted in the hotel room. But then G-Rollin' didn't come good on his end of the bargain. He told me he needed one more thing and I went to tell him it was his turn to act…but I was wrong. Of course he never planned on carrying it out."

Theresa got a faraway look in her eyes and took another drag on her cigarette. "I swear, when they were fucking me the whites of their eyes turned red, Tommy."

When Theresa and I got together, it was awful from the start. Neither one of us had a home. We were both ending a horrific year of methamphetamine and alcohol abuse, dealing with the ramifications of suicide, and juggling our individual issues. She trusted me and I soon met her family. We moved in together with an old friend after a short time. I turned myself in for outstanding warrants again and was locked away for a few more weeks. During that time I was transferred from L.A. County Detention Center to Wayside Minimum Security and on the bus-ride over all of us prisoners listened to the infamous O.J. Simpson car chase over the radio. It was further evidence of the fucking corrupt nature of life.

After that stint I took a job working graveyard shift and started to get clean a few months at a time. We rented a little guest house in Chatsworth and I tried to build a normal life with Theresa. I paid our bills and showed up to work each night. It was my first steady job expediting film at a film lab on Sunset Boulevard. I loved Theresa to death, but when I think of it now I cared for her more like a daughter. I wanted to protect her. But I, too, was incapable of being content and living a normal life. All the while, she shared her ideas with me and more and more I began to recognize what everyone else had seen. They'd all told me she was crazy and had a tendency toward drama. It wasn't long before her mental instability ignited my own obsession with death and darkness and that instability became most of what we shared.

One morning I returned home from work to Theresa screaming at me. I couldn't make heads or tails of her accusations before she fled to the bedroom, locked the door, and screamed that she was calling 9-1-1. I sat and waited for the cops while she raved inside the room. She reported to them that she was convinced I was going to attack her, but when the police asked her if I'd ever been physically violent with her in the past, she said no and could not give them any specific reason why she thought I might have done so that morning. Afterward she apologized profusely and told me it was all in her head. She was sorry, I didn't deserve it, and she'd make it up to me. Even her delusions, though, started to rub off on me.

It wasn't long after that when she started acting strange and I started eavesdropping on her phone conversations. One day we fought and I went to my parent's house. Theresa called me later in the day to ask me to meet her somewhere. She was acting strange. I asked her why she wanted me to meet her and she wouldn't say. By that time, I'd convinced myself that she was going to have me killed. Maybe she'd found another gang-banging pimp to take me down. I wrote a good-bye note on the wall of my parent's garage and drove off to meet my death.

It didn't come for me, but darkness continued to surround us and I felt it encroaching ever more on my fragile sense of stability. We started to get algae and mold spores in the bathroom and I complained to the landlord who owned the adjacent house, but to no avail. I became furious and ripped the toilet out and threw it in the yard. I told him we'd use his toilet until he saw fit to do something about getting us a new one and for several weeks we did just that. I was obsessed with being right and I'd never really operated that way before.

Life with Theresa was totally unmanageable on my own, so I started going to twelve-step meetings again. My survival instincts pushed me once more and I started attending the Little Brown Church for 7 a.m. meetings. On a March morning in 1995, after a meeting, I met Mick Denali. He didn't look to be anything special in the midst of Studio City, California. But he was outgoing, smart, and enthusiastic about the recovery program he ran across the street and I really connected with him. I started hanging out at The Recovery House on Moorpark Street where he was the manager and all of a sudden I had a new sobriety date and a whole new outlook.

With my newfound strength, Theresa's neurosis found little to feed off of and we grew apart. She moved back in with her dad and I finally got out of the guest house where so much dysfunction had taken place. When I left, the toilet was still resting on its side in the yard.

Over the years, I would go to meetings here and there. A couple of times I went because I got ordered by the court. Other times it was out of some misguided instinct for self-preservation. But I always viewed it as a sort of social club where I could go for support as needed. I would stay clean for a while and still not get what it was about at all.

Only in 1995 when I met Mick D., did I learn that recovery programs were a place to stop and learn and seek more. The most sobriety I ever had prior to that was nine months. In that time, I had seen glimpses of a world that was greater than the one I lived in. I felt the presence of God and saw the possibility for a new life. The feeling was out of this world, but I was scared of it, too, and I never believed that I could hold on to it. I didn't know what was wrong with me and why I couldn't get it. But I realize now that I was always trying to take control. I would take a small step forward, think I was good to go, and say, "Thanks, God, but I'll take it from here."

Mick was enthusiastic about recovery and God as a solution to our healing. There were ten guys in the House and they would share their stories with each other right in front of me, opening their souls to a stranger, and that gave me a strong dose of what recovery was all about. It taught me a lot and I'd never really been a part of anything like that before. I'd always had a chip on my shoulder and thought I was somehow better than the rest of the people in the room. But at The Recovery House a whole new world opened up to me. I saw how recovery was a way of life, not just a dose of healing here or there. And it was a lot of fun! I really started opening up and Mick became my first sponsor. He took me through the steps. The fifth step was to share with the others and I finally began to talk about things I previously thought I would hold inside me till I died. I began to see that there was an explanation for what was happening to me and that the real problem was in the way I thought about things. But most importantly, I began to see that there was a solution. We went to the beach, movies, meetings and picnics. There was always plenty to do and it was exciting and positive and motivating.

Mick was from South Boston and he had some friends come out to visit occasionally. The one who I really connected with was Alex Garza. He was a really well-rounded guy who'd done several years in prison. He was a jewelry thief. That Christmas, Mick invited me to go to Boston with him and I agreed. I was twenty-six years old and that was my first paid vacation ever.

When we got back I continued working the graveyard shift with the aid of endless supplies of cigarettes and coffee. I was feeling pretty good and recovery was helping me learn how to assert myself with girls and even face rejection without being totally devastated. By that time, Mick had introduced me to a whole new spiritual life and a God I had never known. I was about six months clean then, but still too comfortable in Hollywood at night. I had always prided myself on never having to pay for sex. Fueled by machismo, I used that claim to bolster my ego. But in my new sober state I was fueled by boredom and had no fear of mixing with people. My high ideals changed quickly when I started asserting myself with hookers.

Sport-fucking became my new drug of choice. I thought—or at least tried to tell myself—that I was just healthy and horny, enjoying my new life of sobriety. The truth was that I was still trying to fill that hole inside of me and share some dysfunctional love with broken women who were sexually abused, like me. Fortunately Mick stressed confession in his program through the fourth and fifth steps, so I was able to let go of most of the guilt and shame of being with those hookers. I reasoned with myself that it made sense not to lead girls on, or hurt myself by pandering my emotions. Instead, I opted for the clean transaction. Guilt and shame still ate at me like a cancer, though. What was wrong with me, I wondered? Why did I get so much joy out of the things that I knew I would hate myself for later?

I was living with my parents then and I talked to Theresa for the first time in a long while. I had always felt bad about leaving her and there was guilt there, too. But she seemed to be doing better. We had a few laughs and then she told me she had bought a mailing franchise with her dad and brother and was helping run it. She told me often about the crazy stuff people tried to ship.

"Right now we have a couple pounds of weed sitting here and we don't know what to do with it."

Mick had two years of sobriety but he was still a hustler. When I told him about this later he said, "You know what we've gotta do, right?"

He swore that we could make $500 easily by taking a trip back east to deliver it. I talked Theresa into letting us have the weed. A week later, we paid her a few hundred bucks for the load.

Within weeks we were flying back with ten pounds, thirty pounds, then forty-five pounds. We were making easy money, but it came with a penalty. We started travelling as much as twice a week. I quit my regular job and lost all sense of structure in my daily life. I didn't even know what day it was most of the time because my schedule was so crazy. We started taking as much as we could carry, which was about fifty-five pounds at most, wrapped in clothing inside suitcases and duffle bags. It nearly drove me crazy when I made the occasional trip by myself, waiting at baggage claim for the cops to descend at any moment. But the most painful part about traveling was seeing the families. They would be going on vacation, getting through life together. And I was alone, smuggling drugs and heading for prison any minute. This was not what I got sober and went through all that shit for. It was nerve-wracking as hell and not very conducive to a spiritual life.

The scariest part by far was grabbing the bags off the carousel in Boston. Especially after flying all night on a red-eye. Every look, every movement around us sent up a flare of paranoia. The anticipation was nauseating as we waited for the bags to come around. If we waited too long it was just us and the bags, and the threat of discovery mounted.

I decided to get a place with Dean, who had been in The Recovery House with me. He was a simple guy and he'd been living in the L.A. Mission for a year before entering The Recovery House and then moving into the place on Hazeltine and Moorpark with me. He was a recovering crackhead and he loved music from bands like The Pixies and Urge Overkill. Around that time I got really into hockey and managed to buy some great hockey skates and gear with all the cash I was making from the "export" business. Hockey was where I was getting some much needed exercise and focus.

I was two years sober in 1998 and Mick and I were making another trip to Boston. While we were there we caught up with some of our buddies and made time to go to meetings to support our recovery. Since we'd been doing the same thing for over a year I was now friends with a lot of the guys there. It was summer and I walked in late to a Sunday night Southie Kids meeting on Dorchester and Vinton Street. There was an empty seat in the front left corner of the room, next to Ben Lucci. I tried to sit down quietly and say hi to Ben, who was surprised and excited to see me.

Once I settled in, I attempted to subtly scan the room while still being considerate to the speaker. The room was full of about thirty people and of these there were a few cute girls, but one stood out more than all the others. She was sitting about nine chairs over from me in the front row. She had beautiful fair skin, high cheekbones and dark, shoulder-length hair that was cut in an edgy, punk style. I could tell she was tall and admired her posture. But her eyes were teasing me. She kept them forward, attentive to the speaker, and it drove me crazy that they were eluding me. I nudged Ben.

"Who's that?"

He leaned forward and raised an eyebrow at me.

"Arlene Ryan."

Throughout the rest of the meeting, I didn't retain a single thing that was said. How could I? I was fantasizing about being outside after the meeting and talking to Arlene. I imagined her saying, "Oh, you're from Hollywood?" and "Oh, you're a drummer, too?" I imagined the luxury of looking into her eyes freely...

None of this happened. When the meeting let out we were all kind of standing around outside on the steps of Fourth Street Presbyterian Church socializing, but Arlene Ryan was nowhere in sight. Instead, Mick met a girl named Julia Malloy who was a good friend of Alex's. Alex was doing prison time again, but he'd always told me what a great girl Julia was if I ever got a chance to meet her. I stood to the side, smoking while she and Mick hit it off. I couldn't have been less happy for them. I was leaving Boston tomorrow and only one thought excluded all others—I had to meet Arlene Ryan.

One good thing had come of my attentiveness that

night and this I clung to even as the airplane hurtled me back to L.A.: As we were standing to exit the meeting, Arlene had looked up briefly and I had seen that her eyes were a deep and intoxicating shade of green.

CHAPTER NINE

2013

It was my mother who asked, "Should we come out...and go with you?"

I could hear the trepidation in her voice. Having told them about the meeting I would be going to with the Church's representative and attorney, I didn't expect them to like the idea let alone offer to join me. It was another hesitant gesture though, which was slightly more characteristic. I'd spent many years in recovery learning to be open and to invite the openness of others. So I saw this as an opportunity and I grabbed it.

"Aw, man. If you guys are serious it would mean the world to me if you were here."

There was silence on the other end. My dad cleared his throat.

"Of course, of course," he said.

After a long silence, my mother spoke again.

"We've always tried to be there for you, Tommy."

The thing is, I know they have. They've done it in their own way, but it's no less valid an attempt than what someone else might have done. It may not have been right. It may not have been what I needed, but they tried. And

I've forgiven everyone else for not being able to save me. I've learned the importance of saving myself.

When I got off the phone with my parents I called my friend Paul, an insurance agent and one of the greatest supporters of what I was doing. He agreed to join us in the meeting between the representatives of the Church and myself. So we waited for the day to come and I imagine for everyone but me it was like waiting for a trip to the gallows. I was rather looking forward to a chance—any chance—to be heard.

The day of our scheduled meeting was a scorcher. The church had sent Henry Scheffer who was one of the attorney's from Kirton McConkie. Henry's had been the signature that adorned our correspondence thus far with the lawyers for the church. He was a made man for the church mafia as far as I could tell.

Of the friends who I'd told about my case, they all advised me not to make a move without an attorney. But deep down I believed that no one could represent my case better than myself. After my experiences with Moore, I was even more disenchanted with the idea of attorneys. I felt they only wasted time and fluffed things up to see how they'd pay off, then opted for the quickest resolution if the profit margin wasn't high enough. So, there I was ready to head into the lion's den without anything to represent me but the God-awful truth.

I had so much nervous energy on the day of the meeting. Arlene and I met with my parents and Paul at our house and we caravanned to the Scottsdale Marriott. It was 117 degrees and I was wearing a dress shirt and slacks. I was hot and full of stress. But Arlene was there squeezing my hand. My parents were present and unreadable and Paul was relaxed and professional.

Henry was joined by Rod Carpenter who was an attorney for Latham and Watkins, a California firm subcontracted by Kirton-McConkie to add perspective since the case originated in that state and would be governed by California law. And to think I started the whole process believing that I could resolve the issue face to face with the church leaders themselves. I should have known they don't make a move without sending in their henchmen. I smirked a little as I thought of this and looked at my own motley crew of supporters. My mother was sitting upright, dressed in her Sunday best alongside my father who already looked like he'd gone nine rounds with a worthy opponent. Paul assumed an air of confidence and Arlene smiled at me nervously. With that I felt all of the pent up stress diminish and I was ready to take this on.

Henry and Rod introduced themselves to me first and then immediately narrowed their eyes on Paul.

"Who do we have here?"

"This is my friend Paul."

"Attorney?"

"Insurance agent."

They extended a handshake, sizing Paul up. Paul's a sharp guy and I could tell they didn't like him right away. They moved on.

My parents greeted the two men as warmly and falsely as if they were meeting any members of the church. Of course they knew mutual people and my dad mentioned an association they shared which immediately opened a cordial conversation between the four of them that caused Arlene and I to raise our eyebrows at each other. I felt like breaking up their little *tete-a-tete* by reminding them that this was not a Sunday service, but I kept my cool. That was going to be my biggest challenge I knew, but I was determined to make it through the meeting without raising my voice or letting anger win.

Finally we got down to business.

"So, Mr. Womeldorf, what are you looking for? What do you want from us?"

"I want what I deserve: to be heard and to be compensated fairly. I want an apology from the Church."

Henry blandly jotted notes on his notepad.

We got into evidence then and they asked me to share with them what happened. I saw my parents sort of shrivel as I shared the details of the sex abuse, the denial by the church, and the subsequent years of drug and alcohol abuse. The attorneys listened and took notes. Other than that there was no show of emotion, no surprise.

They broke off my speech at only one point. Henry Scheffer looked up sharply when I said, "The church knew, too, that Craig Mathias was a sexual predator and that he had even been sent home from his mission for inappropriate behavior."

"Where did you get that information?"

"Craig told me himself while he was trying to ingratiate himself to me, while he was grooming me to be his victim. He said the church sent him home but he got away with it—whatever he did."

"That's a pretty loose association."

"It's still an association."

"You say you don't know what it was that he did. It seems to me you're making some pretty irresponsible accusations. You have very little to support them."

"Well that's the point, isn't it? I'm telling you what I know and relying on you to make the connections, check the records, and realize that I'm right."

The henchmen smirked. Still, I found it interesting that

they chose to argue that one point instead of the many others, as if they knew it was the one hole in my case, or perhaps the one hole in theirs. They knew that if something on this was in their records--whether truth or lie--it would be impossible for me to prove otherwise. Still, they spoke with an arrogance that told me exactly who had the upper hand.

"The fact is, Mr. Womeldorf, you're claiming these things happened to you and yet none of it was ever reported."

"You're telling me what you think happened. That's not a fact. I reported Craig's sexual abuse in a meeting between Bishop Brent Griffith's, my father, and myself in 1983. Nothing was done. I'm not surprised there's no record of it."

"You say your father was present at that meeting?"

"He was."

Henry looked to Rod.

"Do you recall this incident?" he asked my father. "Do you specifically remember reporting these claims to Bishop Griffith's in 1983?"

My father looked down at his hands in his lap. He looked tortured and I could see that he was conflicted by emotions.

"No, I don't remember."

Arlene's and my jaws dropped simultaneously. My ears rang and I felt like I was in a vacuum. I couldn't believe it. That one meeting when I was thirteen years old had been the axis around which my entire life had spun and my father didn't even remember it. He looked at me and I stared at him, dumbfounded. He just kind of shrugged and went back to examining his hands. His mind must have been in turmoil, unable to just stop and rest on the truth even for a moment. It was as if the turmoil happened by default, a sure enough method of denial.

Finally, the attorneys addressed the fact that they had made me an offer six months prior to this.

"Which was more or less a slap in the face," I said, "The offer indicated an acknowledgment of wrongdoing but placed a value on that offense that hardly covers the pain the Church has caused. They do this sort of thing...buying people's silence; sweeping things under the rug. But eventually they have to be accountable. Eventually the truth comes to light. I won't disappear. I won't be silent."

"There is a standard amount we pay out to victims. Asking for more is taking a shot in the dark. I can't say that I see it going well. You've given us very little to go on."

Rod smiled a weak smile and I could see that he was pleased with the way things were going. Henry tapped his pencil on the table.

"It seems to me you pay too little, too late. Doesn't that bother you at all?"

My temper was mounting but I knew I had to keep it under wraps. Paul had coached me well and stressed that they would dismiss me entirely at the first sign of hostility. Instead I tried to calm myself and be likeable. At least I'd always been good at that.

"Well, we're offering to settle this now, but the amount hasn't changed."

I sat there for a moment, processing this.

"You know, in the course of my life there are victims of abuse all around me. Most of them would be willing to use some quick compensation to inebriate themselves. I would have, at one time. But that's just because I wouldn't see the truth, just like you're unwilling to see it now. What you're offering is not enough. It's just not enough."

The two men on the other side of the table looked at each other. I saw my parents shift in their seats. Henry closed his file folder resolutely and began to gather his things.

"Mr. Womeldorf, the best advice I have for you is to hire a lawyer. Otherwise you'll never be satisfied. With an attorney at least you'll be able to sleep at night knowing that you did all you could. In the meantime, we'll put together what we have and we'll be in touch with you."

That was it. The way Henry said it told me that he knew as well as I did that my file would go back to the office, be evaluated as to how much of a threat my claims were worth and duly pushed aside as worthless. I had been in that seat before, sitting across from Bishop Griffith's while he determined my own worth. Hadn't I lived my life in that image of worthlessness for years? What was left for me now, if they turned me away again?

"I'm writing a book," I said.

Rod raised his eyebrow. Henry's pencil stopped mid-tap.

"If I can't make the church acknowledge the truth I can at least show the rest of the world how actively the church is trying to hide it."

"And what do you want from us? Help with writing it?" Rod said, resuming his cockiness.

Rod was clearly the bad cop here, which made sense. He was trying to intimidate me but I was exhilarated. I had seen the brief hesitations, the fears, the weaknesses of the Church's henchmen. I knew then that whatever the outcome of my case, I would be writing—sharing my story with the others out there who have also been forsaken by those who hardly practice what they preach.

Outside, the heat revitalized me and I felt that I could finally breathe. I was proud. I was full of the feeling of possibility even though everyone around me was exhausted. We all lingered for a moment in the parking lot and my dad approached me.

"Listen, son, I'm sorry. I wasn't as focused as you were in there. I probably haven't ever been as focused as you." He seemed to be at a loss for words. "I'm just really sorry if I let you down."

I looked at him for a moment, that aging man who had the years written on his face. I imagined his inner struggle had been more than he was been willing to bear at times, as it is for all of us. I realized then that he probably blocked the events of that day out. We tend to bury the past when it's too painful to revisit. I've been able to revisit mine, through years of therapy and support, but so many people don't ever get the courage to face the pain. I was able to see then the perfect beauty of humanity. It's as if I was able to see a glimpse of myself thirty or forty years in the future, with one of our daughters standing in judgment of me. It was clear as crystal. And I leaned on love and forgiveness.

"We just show up and do our best, Dad. It's not your fault."

I hugged him and my mom.

Everyone else was burned out but I felt like I could run a marathon. When all was said and done, I had the attorneys in that room for an hour and a half. I had been able to hold their attention and listen and be heard. They might have seen it as a success on their side of the table, but I couldn't help but believe that everything would work out in the end. I felt empowered. Before I even set foot in the door that night, I started to think again of Dan Fasy. I now knew that I needed to get the best lawyer I could.

When we arrived home, the girls swarmed on me and Arlene smiled across their heads at me. Everything else vanished with the love in that house. My parents took us out to dinner at a barbecue restaurant. I kept looking around the table at my family, and in particular at the woman who had enchanted me so many years before. My heart swelled for Arlene and for the life that we'd built. That was June 19th, 2013 and it was our nine year wedding anniversary.

CHAPTER TEN

1998 – 1999

The thought of her excluded all others. I talked to Alex the following day, after the plane landed in Los Angeles. He told me all about Arlene and said she was a great girl. I had always been relentless when I clung to an idea, and I clung to the idea of her for many years after that.

In the meantime, the smuggling jobs were adding up to financial success but emotional upheaval. Alex came out to spend a few months in Los Angeles and it turned out he had grown up with Mark Wahlberg and his family. Mark was in the middle of filming "Boogie Nights" at the time and Alex called him up and we went to his house one night. He lived right above Sunset, near Larabee, in a nice house with an elevator. Mark took us out to dinner that night at The Beverly Club. It was a little ritzy for my taste, but Mark was nice and carried himself like a big superstar.

Meanwhile, our repeated successes in the smuggling business were helping my own ego to grow uncontrollably. By that time, it was no longer just weed that we were moving, but cocaine too. That happened against my will, but the money it brought certainly didn't hurt. Still, there was part of me that knew this was bad news and I tried to start separating myself from the business. At that point, one of the guys in our group was robbed of about $50,000 worth of coke and things got pretty hairy for a while. While I was in Los Angeles, the buyers confronted me about where their cocaine was and I kept my mouth shut. That gave me a lot of credit in Boston afterward.

While on one of the trips to Boston, Mick D. was really discontent and tossing around the idea of drinking. It affected me because I loved and respected him. I saw his pain and felt it as my own. Without the guidance of people like Mick, my life had no meaning or direction. For the next two days, Mick bounced like a pinball around Boston and left me alone with the ghost of what he'd said. My sadness turned to anger as I realized that his words had been the catalyst for me to start toying with the idea myself.

When we got back on the plane, I was uncomfortable in his presence and he didn't even notice. He started talking again about how much he wanted a drink. I decided then and there to pay him back for what he'd done. The next time the stewardess came by I ordered a Bacardi and Coke.

"What are you doing, man?"

"I'm doing what you threatened to do. You can't go around saying things like that and not recognize the impact they have. I've been obsessing about having a drink ever since you started tossing the idea around."

I poured the entire contents of the tiny bottle of Bacardi into the plastic soda cup and mixed it. My life was out of sorts anyway. It just made more sense to get through the days with the help of alcohol. I tossed half the drink back.

"I can't believe you're doing this."

"Hey, Mick, you always told me alcohol was nothing to joke about. Then you went and broke the golden rule. At least I had the courage to do it and not just talk about it."

Mick shook his head and didn't talk to me for the rest of the flight. Mick lasted another three weeks in sobriety and in that time we would talk only occasionally.

"So, how's drinking treating you?"

"It's great!" I answered spitefully.

And the thing is, it *was* great in the beginning. Whenever I got back into drinking and drugs, the fall happened slowly. I would start out casually, sure that I could control the allergy this time. I started hanging out with my drinking friends again. We'd go out to eat at Los Toros Mexican restaurant before going to the Candy Cat strip club next door. We would haunt the Sagebrush bar in Calabasas. Those guys could drink and they loved hanging out with me because I was fun and reckless. After a while, they must have realized that I never went home after a night of partying with them. If I didn't pass out in my car, I would make it to a darker friend's house, or head downtown to score some coke and heroin.

Mick and I were still making the occasional exporting trip so money was still coming in. I was spending it as quick as I made it. At about 2:00 one morning we were closing down the Sagebrush and met two bimbos as we were leaving. I started talking to them of course, looking for somewhere to go to continue the madness. My other friends were content to make it home and wake up to their lives the following day, but not me. Every moment or hour was the only one I had that meant anything to me at all. I remember hoping many nights that it would be my last. I wondered, as I had in high school, what would happen if I died in a strange girl's house or in a ditch on the side of the road? Would people actually be moved to care? Wouldn't they wonder, then, what had gone wrong with me?

One of the two girls was hotter than the other. The other was not bad looking, but she was definitely overshadowed by her better-looking friend. I decided to go with the sure thing and talked more with the less attractive girl.

"It's my friend you want to be with," she said after a few minutes, as if she could see right through me.

I laughed, caught off guard.

"Your friend looks great but she's probably a lot of drama. You seem more low-key and you look great yourself."

She laughed. "You're full of shit."

Her name was Carrie and I warmed up to her low self-opinion. There was something I understood! I told the girls I had some really good weed in my Jeep and we went to a park to smoke some of it. I was right and Carrie's friend turned out to be a basket case. She was talking about some stupid drama and she had a kid. Even I could see how messed up that was. It didn't stop me from wanting to nail her, but I sure didn't want to get mixed up with her. At the end of the night—or morning—Carrie gave me her number, still insisting that it was pointless since I obviously would rather be with her friend.

A couple of weeks prior, my roommate Dean and I confessed to each other that we had relapsed. It turned out we both fell back to drinking at about the same time. Not long after I met Carrie, Dean and I were hanging out for a night of heavy drinking and we decided to take a trip to Mexico. Dean loved the weed and was a laid back guy. We set out on our trip and stopped in a border town to get more beer. After getting hammered there, we decided to walk across the border, get some coke, and walk it back to our motel room. It seemed like a perfectly good idea to me.

We found an eightball of coke right away in Mexico, tasted it, and set out to walk back across the border. That's when I saw the German Shepherds. Holy shit! I tensed up and Dean started freaking out next to me, saying there was no way we could get past the dogs. I thought I shoved the coke far enough up my ass but Dean was really bringing doubt.

"Shut up," I hissed, "I'm the one holding it!"

We ran the gauntlet and I probably said something funny and totally inappropriate to the border guards. That's always been my style, trying to lighten the mood and loosen myself and everyone else up. It was incredibly intense, but we made it. It was a similar rush to waiting at the baggage claim for a suitcase full of drugs, or picking up a hooker. It crossed my mind that every instance was probably furthering my addiction to the rush, but that was no good reason to stop.

When we got back to our hotel room, I started to realize that something was wrong. Aside from the fact that I always had to take a shit before doing coke, I soon realized there was no sandwich baggie in my ass. I couldn't believe I dropped it somewhere. I went out and told Dean and he was even more disbelieving. In fact, he got this skeptical look in his eyes and started questioning my story.

"You think I'm gonna sneak in the tiny fucking bathroom and do it all without you? I'm not lying, man."

"No. Alright. We gotta go back and look for it then."

There's a certain code, even among drug addicts, and we wouldn't have tried to put anything past each other. We backtracked all the way to the guard station at the crossings, but had no luck. With no other options, we just smoked a ton of weed and drank ourselves to sleep. Coming off of sobriety, it was still new enough to both of us that we could get by on that alone.

Looking forward to Mexico, we woke up and drove down to Rosarito. Dean didn't have a lot of money, but he didn't know about the smuggling action I'd been seeing either, so I just told him I had some extra cash and got us a nicer hotel room in Rosarito. In the bars that night there were teenage girls drinking in the bar and Dean and I were both looking forward to getting laid by whatever means possible. Drunk American teenagers, old nasty Mexican hookers, it didn't matter. We were pigs in addiction.

Only one thing called to us more than sex and that was drugs. We started asking around and learned that the best place to get coke was Tijuana, which was about an hour away by taxi so we decided that I would make the trek. I jumped in a station wagon with the word "Taxi" on the side and asked the driver to get me to Tijuana for some coke.

"Yeah!" he said, nodding enthusiastically.

I felt like I had to shit already! The driver started up some back roads through the mountains, picking up other people. It was dark out then and I started freaking out. Nobody spoke English and there wasn't room for another body in the station wagon. I was squished in the middle of the back seat, chain smoking and asking everyone if they were going to Tijuana.

We finally made it and emptied people out one by one. We got our coke—this time a quarter ounce—and the driver told me he had to hold it in case we got pulled over. That was fine except I was dying to do some already. We got back to Rosarito safely and I threw the driver a tip and headed back to our room. Dean was pacing he was so freaked out.

"That took you forever!" He said when he saw me and I could tell he was relieved that I hadn't been hauled away to Mexican jail and that I had the coke.

"You're telling me. I haven't even sniffed any yet!"

We stayed up the rest of the night. Dean got all fucked up and paranoid and went into the bathroom with a goatee and came out with nothing but a mustache. I started laughing.

"Dean! You look different on coke!"

He was trying to act normal, like nothing had changed. "What do you mean?"

"You look like a cop!"

"Shut up! I fucked up shaving."

Well, I messed with him for the rest of the trip telling him we'd never be able to score drugs now.

The next day, we made our way to some pharmacies. I was dying to get my hands on some morphine, Dilaudid, or even Demerol. We went through the procedure, which means going around the corner to talk to a doctor and get a prescription for twenty dollars. It was basically the same routine as in L.A. but for a lot less bullshit and money. So, I told the doctor I was on vacation and my back was killing me. The best he could do was get me some Percocet, Percodan, and Vicodin. They were high milligram pills but didn't seem very potent so I started taking them by the handful. Dean got Ritalin, which is like pharmaceutical speed, and ended up with enough to keep us both up for the next couple months.

Once we were back home I called Carrie and started

hanging out with her again. The first day she came back to the house with me we walked in and Dean was sitting at the coffee table all Ritalined out with the bong sitting in front of him. He had this puzzled look on his face when he saw us because he hadn't slept in a couple days. It was kind of embarrassing to bring a new girl home to that.

I knocked his feet off of the coffee table and said, "C'mon, man, act like you got something else going on, please!"

After that we mostly hung out at Carrie's apartment in Tarzana. She was pretty cool, but more of an artsy, wine-drinking hippie type. I was eating tons of pills and chipping with heroin and coke and before long Carrie started making comments. She wasn't enjoying all of my partying as much as I was. I started to get in the old, fallback mindset again that it was her problem if she didn't like me the way I was. Why were girls never happy? I took her to dinner, spent money on her, but now she wanted me coherent 24/7 too?

"Didn't we meet at a bar, drinking and smoking drugs?" I asked her one night when she laid into me. She didn't like that too much.

"Sure, but that isn't all there is to life!" she hollered.

Could have fooled me.

We planned a trip to Seattle, just her and I. The first few days were great and we hung out in the Central Tavern and got to see all of the places where my idol, Andy Wood, had been. They had some great jazz downtown in a hippie neighborhood. Carrie taught me how to find the best bars in town by hopping in a taxi and telling them to take us where the locals go instead of the usual tourist traps. In Seattle, this brought us to some old dive bar near the ferry terminals. We sat there staring out at the water and I thought that Andy must have used those ferries a lot being from Bainbridge Island which was just out across the water.

The next day, we headed for another port that connects to Victoria, BC by ferry. I smuggled some pills and weed across the Canadian border, less than two weeks after my Mexican adventure. But it wasn't like I could just walk through life on my own power. By that time I had the added misery of knowing that my dreams of being a taken-care-of rock star were pretty much dead in the water at the ripe old age of twenty-eight. All the great rockers are usually dead by twenty-seven anyway, right? I had over-lived my time.

We got a room in a nice hotel in Victoria and had some fun that night. At the first bar we walked into some guy offered me high-grade weed straight out of the gate. I was flattered, but was also sure it was a setup. That guy was either a cop or wanted to fuck in the bathroom. I took the safe bet and let him give me some for later. Canadians seemed to be really nice, hard-working people and we even saw some beautiful hookers on our walk back to the hotel.

The next morning was when things took a bad turn. I woke up to find Carrie pacing at the foot of the bed with her arms crossed. It was several bleary moments before I realized she was actually talking to me.

"Are you just going to sleep? I really want to get out and do things, Tommy."

"Have you lost your fucking mind? Why don't you go for a walk or something?"

I covered my head with the pillow and she was tugging at it in the next instant.

"Get away from me!" I yelled. Who did she think she was, a supermodel or something? I paid for a nice vacation and she couldn't even let me sleep in?

That pretty much convinced me it was time to part

ways with Carrie. As soon as we got back home I just stopped hanging out with her and stopped calling. About a week later she came by my friend's house looking for me. We were on the front porch when she walked up saying she needed to talk to me.

"Oh, Tommy, your mom's looking for you," the guys teased.

"I told her to come by," I lied.

It was pretty embarrassing. I went back to her house with her and tried to end things and leave, but she wasn't having any of it. I was walking to the car and she started pushing me around, trying to get a rise out of me or start a fight. I've never been much for play fighting because I tend to go straight to rage. She got in my face one more time and I pushed her backwards. She fell down in the grass and looked up at me with this dramatic look, sitting there in the middle of her complex. I'd had enough.

"Do yourself a favor," I said, "Stay down there and let me leave."

And there went another failed relationship. What was wrong with me? Was every attempt I ever made at having a relationship just a charade to get sex? Maybe.

A few weeks later I met a sexy, exotic girl named Marcia at the same bar. She turned out to be a psychologist, and Jewish. I had been drinking like a fish all day on a Hell's Angels Poker Run and was borrowing a friend's 1200 Sportster. All the alcohol (and heroin on the sly), along with the support of the friends around me got my confidence soaring high enough to pursue her. Otherwise I would have been smart enough to know she was out of my league.

I ended up taking off with Marcia on the back of the bike and we pulled over somewhere along the way to make out. That was all fun but somewhere I dimly remembered that I was supposed to be at work on Gower and Sunset developing film. My shift started at 10:00 p.m. on Sunday night and it was now 1:00 on Monday morning. I dropped Marcia off and called work to tell them some lie about being in an accident and having to go to the hospital. I got to work by 2 a.m. and went through the rest of my shift mostly in a blackout.

For the next few weeks I hung out with Marcia and tried to hide my heroin habit. I tried to kick it and when she came around I told her I had the flu but it wasn't contagious. I just wanted to be held by her and told that I would be okay. She gave me that at least and I was grateful. But all the while I was wondering why I loved and needed women so much. Why was I so sexually perverted and how would I ever be better than I was?

Marcia wasn't one to show her cards and if she suspected I was using heroin she didn't let on. I continued to use on the sly, getting Mexican Black Tar from Bonnie Brae Street. When you smoked it it smelled like burnt dog food. I didn't know it at the time because I was obviously still immature when it came to relationships, but Marcia probably found it easy to overlook much of my behavior. She was newly separated from her husband and it took me many years of looking back on that time in my life to recognize that she'd been using me as a tool to get back at this guy. She took me to meet him once, dragging me along knowing full well that it would stir up trouble. I played right into her hands, getting all riled up and wanting to beat him up. I made it easy for her. Even in the condition I was in, I always wondered why she was with me. It was clear she didn't feel the same way about me as I felt about her. But I subjected myself to the listless love of women never knowing what real love even was. When we parted ways, Marcia didn't even care. I said some horrible things to her because I was hurting and I realized that was always my response: to hurt others when I was deeply hurt.

After that I met Carmela. She was more my style: a crack-whore from Hollywood. She just walked right up to my car and who was I to turn her away? We started seeing each other. She was from Minneapolis and had gone to college intermittently there. She was one of the most functionally confused people I'd ever met, but in my delusions I still believed she could be the one to save me. And so she became the next person I anchored myself to.

One night I was partying with some of the boys from Boston who were in town and Ben Lucci and I decided to go cop some heroin but realized we didn't have any needles. We started walking the boulevard to find some and it was pure chance that I saw Carrie across the street. I didn't want to see her, but I remembered that she was getting into nursing just before we ended things. I approached her and introduced her to Ben. She seemed uneasy at first, but it's always been my way to disarm people and she was probably easier than most because of her low opinion of herself. We went back to her apartment and I started sniffing around for supplies only to find two huge needles. I was scared to death to use the things, but beggars can't be choosers so I stuffed them into my pockets and made some excuse for why we had to leave so quickly.

After a couple days of using the sword-like needles, we acquired some insulin points. I'd been drinking heavy all day and Ben cooked two balloons. I wasn't operating on the best judgment and decided to blast a whole one in one shot. It was more than I'd ever done and it proved to be more than my overwrought body could handle. I immediately blacked out for a couple of hours and when I came to it was to find myself soaking wet in a bathtub. There were two girls on the floor crying and Ben was splashing me with water. As soon as they saw that I was alive, their fear turned to anger.

"What's the matter with you, Molly?" I said to one of the girls.

"You OD'd you son of a bitch," Ben said, sitting down with his back to the wall.

Apparently, I'd turned blue and he'd called our friends Gail and Molly over. They all thought I was dead or well on my way and Ben confessed that he'd tossed around the idea of throwing me in the dumpster behind the building if I'd died.

"Oh, come on," I said, "You guys are being totally irrational. I have a headache."

I rose from the tub and had to find some dry clothes to wear before heading out to work. Three hours later I was at Culver Studios, at my new job with Four Stone Scenery where we built sets for movies and commercials. I was up in the catwalk working on a set for a stupid Leonardo DiCaprio commercial and had a hell of a hangover. I kept envisioning myself falling sixty feet to the ground below. I could actually see myself laid out on the floor, peacefully removed from the world. It was a tough day of work but I was a warrior and I made it through the long hours of work knowing that as soon as my shift was over I would go out and medicate some more.

I'd known Rich since the fourth grade and we'd never really lost contact except when Andy shunned me for a while for dating Marilyn. Rich had sided with him then but we'd gradually grown close again and he'd watched me float around from one recovery house to another. Rich was a stand-up guy and when he suggested that we get a place together in Hollywood I was ready to jump at the chance. And so we ended up in Pink. Rich was a great friend to me and it only serves to demonstrate how much I valued his friendship that I was distraught when he left for London to visit his sister.

The dark days that followed were some of the hardest I can remember. I was alone in the world. Rich was gone, Carmela was gone, I was living in a void. I arguably always had been, but it had been easy to tether myself to the people around me and feel that I was living some semblance of a life. Now I was cut free, cast adrift. I wanted to die as I never had before. I was in more pain than I'd ever been in—the kind of emotional and physical pain that begged to be suppressed. It was larger than me and always had been. Yet, in the depths of my despair I had a small hope that if so much pain existed inside of me there must be some amount of love that could fix it all.

I stepped out into the blinding sunlight on that fall morning in 1999 and nearly dragged my aching body up the street. I managed to get myself to a 7:15 a.m. men's meeting on Lankershim Boulevard where I met up with Kent who I had previously met through The Recovery House. He saw immediately that I was having a tough time of it again. After the meeting, he pulled me aside.

"I know what you're going through. You need a few more days to detox and I want you to come to my place so we can guarantee that you won't slide back. I want you to go to John and Mitchell and tell them what you need. They've been there too. They can help you."

I just nodded, unable to push myself any further through this life on my own. Kent knew Mitchell—one of my bosses at Four Stone—from meetings. Later that day, he drove me to the Studio so I could talk with them. As recovering addicts themselves, he and John had seen me going in and out while I worked for them. They recognized the signs and so when I approached them they were open and willing to get me the help I needed. That's the great thing about recovery—there's a lot of love there and a little love was all I needed.

Kent lived in Bel-Air with his roommate Kit and he let me stay there, out of his sight for four or five days while I withdrew, sweat, and convulsed on the floor. At one point I was so sick and desperate that I went into the bathroom, got down on my knees at the toilet and begged God to help me.

"Please help me. Please. If you don't do something, I'll be dead by tonight with a needle in my arm and soaked with puke and piss. If you were God, you'd know this."

Kent found me like that and didn't know much about heroin withdrawal so he called on a buddy of his named Dennis. He was a junkie who'd been clean for a few years and he knew I was going through hell. He came over and just talked to me, casually.

"You getting any sleep?"

I shook my head.

"You eating?"

I nodded.

"What are you eating?"

"Kent makes me some fruit smoothies, and juice…vitamins."

133

"Well, shit. No wonder. Your body's freaked out by all the healthy shit. It's looking for a high, so give it one. You need some donuts and ice cream."

He and Kent loaded me up with some junk food and that alone helped immensely. I was able to keep it all down. During the days after that I let Kent take me all over the place. I knew I had to just let the current carry me, but I soon got wiped out on his agenda. He had us headed over to West Hills for a meeting and the last thing I wanted was to be in a big, packed room at a church with a bunch of clean, smiling people, but I could see the value in it. It felt good to be around others who knew my pain. I didn't listen much to the speaker. She seemed to go on forever and all I wanted to do was curl up and lay under everyone's feet. Then, something she said caused me to perk up.

"My life certainly didn't go according to plan. Nothing turned out how it *should* have. But if I had drawn up a plan for my life, I would have cheated myself out of so much of what I have been given in recovery. I have a child I thought I would never be able to have, a happiness that I thought I had no right to. I came to recovery to take care of a drinking problem, but I've been given so much more than just freedom from addiction."

How is it that I had endured forty minutes of nothing but gibberish only to awaken for those few essential sentences? My ears and my heart opened up and I knew then that I had not been wrong. There was hope out there, somewhere. There was such a thing as a love that could heal.

CHAPTER ELEVEN

1999 – 2000

A day later, on November 15, 1999, I got into Acton Recovery Center, north of Los Angeles. There were three pick-up spots around L.A. County and Jake Castillo, who was like a brother to me, drove me to Olive View Hospital in Sylmar where the Acton passenger van made a pick-up every Monday and Wednesday morning. We both cried when he drove away. He knew all of my troubles. The hardest part for me was getting in the van and committing to a long ride up the mountains, not knowing what awaited me. On the bus, an older guy asked me for a couple of cigarettes. I had a carton or so in my bag and gave him some. I didn't mind giving, but I still had that old idea that the second I offered something I would be cleaned out, taken advantage of, and ultimately feel raped.

Acton was the biggest rehab center in the country, with 200 men and 100 women. I was pretty intimidated at first because it was an L.A. County facility, like a detention center but with a loving rehab factor to it. Still, it was hard for me to see that factor through all the scary looking people who'd been sent there from—or instead of—jail. I was placed in Cabin 11, a six-man room. To enter the

135

cabin, there were four concrete steps and then the door. Immediately to the right, in Bed 1, was Patrick, who was a skinny, nappy-haired black kid. He was twenty-six and a crack-head who'd spent the previous years up in Zion and Bryce Canyon working with the forest and ranger facilities. He loved reading and rapping the Bible. Next to him, in the corner, was Robert who was a little white-trash guy with a handlebar mustache. He wasn't real hard or scary, but was the type of guy who seemed like he'd fit in in jail.

In the next corner, Bed 3, was James from Long Beach. He carried himself like he thought he was cool, grungy, and a little crazy. I didn't care for him much because there was no sincere connection between us and that was my only requirement for friendship. He just held himself back like he was too good for the rest of us and finally got booted for using heroin. Robin replaced him. I made a pretty fast connection with Robin, or "Red," who was thirty-eight, black, and stocky. He seemed to go at a slower pace than the rest and I liked that because it was how I naturally was. He just seemed to feel his way through life the same way I did. He was addicted to alcohol and crack.

In Bed 4 was Lenny Ward who was taller than Red and blacker. He had a goatee and yellowish, bloodshot eyes and he didn't say much to me in my first days there, which intimidated me. Lenny was forty-five and the oldest in our cabin, but he was agile. He looked like Dr. J—Julius Erving—and I told him so. He wore jeans and sweaters and dress loafers and always looked like he took a little extra care with his appearance. Lenny and I bonded a lot over the next couple of weeks. We both liked the young preacher named Darwin who guided our Sunday sermons. Darwin looked just like Urkel from T.V. but he was very intelligent and I think he was something of a child prodigy as a reverend. We called him "The Rev." Even Darwin was trying to recover from a crack addiction. Lenny and I had a little disagreement once and he turned our friendship off real quick. He completely ignored me and wouldn't even make eye contact for a week or two. It killed me but I didn't say a word. Then we ran into each other one day on campus and made an attempt to talk. I started tearing up as I apologized and he did too.

In Bed 5, in the last corner and closest to me, was a Mexican gangster kid who thought he was a rapper and was obsessed with his image, trying to dress and act sharp all the time. He couldn't set it all aside for thirty seconds to form any real connection with me or the others so I was never quite comfortable or trusting around him either.

One of the big things in Acton is that they feed you really well. I quickly gained thirty-five pounds and everyone seemed quite happy about that. Lenny told me later that the guys in the cabin thought I had AIDS or something when I first arrived because I was so thin and sick. Besides getting physically healthier, Acton helped knock some of my walls down and I gained some confidence. I was able to stay on good terms with most everyone there and I believed in the goodness of those people I met and learned to follow my heart and God. I may have marched to my own drum, but I stood upright in doing so and kind of became a man up there. One of the only things I did wrong in my time there was cling to the belief (obsession really) that Carmela could fix my problems and my loneliness. She'd since gone back to Minneapolis, which made me wonder what I was missing even more. Carmela was a nice girl with a nice heart, but she couldn't even take care of herself.

My family was all set to come up for my graduation from Acton's program. But, as the day got closer, I began to get anxious. I'd just received a large disability check from the State of California and began to formulate a disjointed and crazy plan to go be with Carmela in Minneapolis. I made the decision to leave early, before graduation. I really just wasn't ready to be so present in my own life. I wasn't prepared for the amount of clarity and openness that it required. My family would be disappointed, but hadn't they always been? The decision to leave was made harder when some of the guys in my cabin got a large group together to try to convince me to stay. They took turns standing up and lovingly talking me out of my insanity. The power of love is nothing short of amazing and I knew I wasn't being smart. Still, the next morning I woke up and boarded the passenger van to Burbank, and freedom.

It was January, 2000, and I took a trip to Minneapolis for a week. Carmela and her mom picked me up at the airport and things went alright for most of the week. The difficulty came on my last night there. We went to a little dive nightclub called First Avenue to see the Long Beach Dub Allstars. I started to get really socially awkward about halfway through the show and decided to throw a few drinks back. I gave into the obsession and the phenomenon of craving was set in motion. There was no going back.

The next night, I arrived at LAX and stopped at a connection's house on my way home to score some dope. He knew I'd been in recovery and it took a lot for me to convince him that I'd already relapsed and that he'd just be saving me a tough trip down to Bonnie Brae Street. He finally gave in and I left with heroin, coke, and a syringe.

I was unable to deal with the reality of life much at all

and I bounced around high for a few weeks. I was driving a brown Oldsmobile Cutlass that I'd bought off of my friend Miles a while back and I'd pull over anywhere on and around Ventura Boulevard to shoot speedballs. I thought for sure my heart was going to explode and almost hoped it would. I would peel off my clothes and squirm around inside the car, convinced the cops were going to close in on me any minute. It was a dark existence, but a familiar one.

I continued talking to Carmela and stoked the fantasy that if we were together I would be alright. Three months passed this way, with me driving to work and fixing speedballs on the highway, before Carmela called to tell me she was pregnant. It wasn't what I wanted, but I dealt with it okay since I was high all the time.

I talked to Kent off and on and ran into his now ex-girlfriend Kit once in a while. She cared about me and was very motherly, sending me letters and snacks when I was in rehab. I was mixed up though, and always thought about being with her even though her attentions were far from sexual. One night she called this big cell phone I had mainly to call drug dealers and talk to Carmela with. She caught me right after a heavy dose and asked me what I was doing. I awkwardly confessed and could barely talk.

"Tommy, you have to throw it all away. Get rid of the drugs. Will you do that?"

"I can't."

"You can, Tommy. Just get rid of it. Throw it away. I can help you. Someone can come help you."

She continued trying to coach me but she was wrecking my high. I eventually hung up on her.

She never talked to me again. Even later, when I'd run into her again, she couldn't even look at me. It hurt me, but I guess I'd hurt her too. Fixing me must have meant more

139

to her than it meant to me.

I was living upstairs at my parent's house then, in my little brother David's old room. One day my mom came out to the garage to find me holding a needle against my arm, ready to shoot up. I couldn't scramble fast enough to remove the evidence and the guilt was probably written all over my face. It was the perfectly wrong snapshot—the one I never wanted my mom to see—but it was also a perfectly accurate picture of what my life had become.

By then I had committed to Carmela and myself that I was going to move out to Minneapolis, buck up and do the right thing. I tried to clean up and be straight with her. I was only about two days clean when I flew out to be with her and I told her how hard it would be. She said I would be okay. Everything would be okay. Her denial was even greater than mine.

For me, it was always exciting to build from nothing. All I needed was a spark. Carmela and the baby gave me that spark of hope. As soon as I arrived, I made a phone call to the local twelve-step program, asking about meetings and making arrangements to be picked up. A few hours later, Carmela was nervous about who might be arriving to take me to the meeting. I told her it was bound to be someone quality.

"How do you know?" she asked.

"Well, it takes a quality person to jump at service like that."

In spite of my attempts to recover, Carmela continued to sneak drinks here and there. She was not only damaging our unborn fetus, but she also had no idea how big the monster of addiction was that she was up against. My own attempts at sobriety were hit and miss. We went back and forth for a few months, with me drinking just to spite her and her drinking to spite me. Neither one of us had the tools to deal with what we were facing.

Carmela started to bleed one morning and I drove her to the hospital. When they were admitting her and taking her information I found out that she was six years older than she'd told me. That should have been a warning if nothing else was.

It didn't take long for the doctors to confirm that she'd had a miscarriage. Sadly, it didn't come as much of a surprise.

We carried on, drinking and smoking crack after that. I started pushing her around because I was so confused and frustrated, not to mention that I'd lost any respect I'd once had for her on account of drinking through her pregnancy. I did the best thing I could do and secretly bought a plane ticket back home in July. The two days leading up to my departure were especially hard because there was a recovery convention in town and there were recovering alcoholics everywhere. I felt alternately ashamed and anxious, wishing to be anywhere but there.

I got home and didn't really know how to feel. The last few months had been like a weird dream. I was back to Simi Valley, back to living with my parents in their new home, farther removed from the city. Margie had a wiry, energetic little friend named Betty who was a manager at Trader Joe's and helped get me a job there. At thirty-one years old, this was my first job dealing with the public.

Glendale was a pretty diverse community in Los Angeles, with a heavy Armenian population. Working in that setting was a trip. My warm personality, offbeat sense of humor, and lust-filled eyes sat well with some of the customers, but not with bossy Betty. She pulled me aside one night and said, "Your gawking at women in the store is not cool."

I was kind of embarrassed but said, "Are they complaining?"

"Well…no."

"Why do you have such a problem with it, then?"

She gave me a professional, corporate reply. In the short time that I'd worked there I made friends with my fellow employees and scored quite a few numbers from female customers who always left with a smile. I moved in with probably the most mischievous guy I worked with. Dante had a two bedroom apartment in Eagle Rock and had actually gone to Hollywood High School with Carmela. I moved into the second bedroom with my futon bed. I wasn't really drinking much at all then, but Dante and I both smoked a ton of cigarettes and loved girls. I even started some community college courses, trying to get my life on a worthwhile path.

It was even better for me because Dante only liked Asian girls, especially Thai. He actually had an order to his preferences that went: Thai, Laotian, Vietnamese, Pilipino, Korean, Japanese, Chinese. I might have bumped Japanese girls up on the list if it were me. He also liked Asian mixed with Spanish or Mexican, but never the latter on its own. Most importantly, he couldn't stand white girls, especially blondes because he thought they were too white, Americanized, and spoiled. All of this meant two things: 1) He pushed all white girls my way, and 2) Asian girls would network pretty quickly and without hesitation. They had a lot of friends! This fucker could speak Thai pretty fluently and he was a rock singer. We would go to Thai restaurants and he would sing Karaoke and then the proprietors would serve us alcohol in tea pots until four or five in the morning.

By New Year's I was drinking like a fish again, blacking out, and doing all the driving. Dante liked to go out in his BMW M3 but had gotten a DUI about six months previous, so what was I to do? Sit home and watch TV or jack off to internet porn? Not a chance.

Prior to this, I had worked out a dumb scam to get a few bucks from K-Mart. I had a buddy who worked there as a security guard who let slip two important facts. He told me that customers who filed a slip and fall claim were written out a neat little check and he told me that the store had a rat problem. Well, this got me thinking. In the end, Rich and I purchased a rat from a local pet store and smuggled it into the local K-Mart. I reached into a shelf, letting the rat free from my sleeve and started to act like the damn thing had bitten me. I cut my finger a little to make the story believable when the employees and managers began to gather around.

After that it was easy enough to turn things over to a lawyer to resolve. Still, the thought of it loomed over me and ate away at me. As if I didn't have enough guilt, I had to continually self-inflict more wounds, bonding myself to the guilt they induced. I told myself that all that mattered was the money, and drugs went a long way toward muting the rest of my disappointment in myself.

When my attorney finally called to tell me K-Mart had settled my claim and a check was waiting for me, I rushed over, grabbed it, and headed to the bank. I thought that maybe now it was all over I might feel better about the whole thing. Money was money, after all. I called Rich and told him our payday had come.

We got $15,000, but you would have thought we hit a jackpot. Within three days I was at the pool hall downtown copping dope. I smoked some on the way to a medical supply in Studio City to pick up some needles. I spent the next few months strung out and falling to pieces. Having a hooker by my side and spending big money on heroin and coke made me feel like the rock star I dreamed of being and not the street creature I was. The Glendale Community College classes I'd started taking only a month before went out the window. I started carrying a needle and spoon in my sock at all times, even to work at Trader Joe's. When I was home alone I was looking at soft porn on Dante's computer for hours. When he was home I was on the road in my car, shooting speedballs somewhere, often naked or only in my underwear.

Nobody, especially Dante, knew the extent of my addiction. I would tell him I was going to a friend's house. I had met a couple different girls from Trader Joe's who I was screwing. This was a favorite pastime of mine. I was making insinuating eye contact and salivating over every female who came through my line at work. Older women, girls, it didn't matter. If I threw out the bait I was bound to get something. One day, Betty approached me at my register looking more than a little disapproving.

"You have a phone call."

I went into the back of the store to pick it up. The girl on the other end said her name was Isabela, she was in the store an hour ago and had been through my line. Did I remember her? Of course I did. And we made a date for that night.

It went on this way for a few more months. I attached

myself to Isabela and spent money like the world was ending. As my habit got worse, it also got more expensive. I was having to meet my connection twenty miles away during a half-hour lunch break from work. I was flying down the freeway, dodging in and out of traffic while shooting up and trying to get back to work on time.

Once I was meeting Chewy, my heroin deliver boy, on a quiet, residential side street in Sherman Oaks. When I arrived there were LAPD cars all over the place, circling the blocks all around me. I was petrified, sure that they were closing in at last. Still, I was extremely conscious that driving away without getting dope was not an option. The only conclusion I came to was that I had to get in, get the dope, and shoot up quickly so that when they arrested me I wouldn't be sick for the ride to jail. I copped, fixed, and somehow made it out of there to fly back on the freeway, late for work again.

When I got back there was more than just the usual stern look and reprimand from Betty waiting for me. Her and another manager, Brent, got together and called me into their office. Instead of playing the usual games, I fessed up. There was always this part of me that wanted help; craved salvation, even. Betty looked shocked beyond measure when I told them, matter-of-factly, that I was addicted to drugs and wanted to get to rehab. Brent nodded, though, and said the company would do everything they could to help me.

"And come on back when you're done," he said, "We'll have a place waiting for you."

Brent was the one who picked me up at Dante's apartment to take me to Tarzana Treatment Center. He was recovering too, and when he got to my room he started rushing me, eager to get out of there because it was such a dark and nasty place. I stalled, shooting dirty cotton water and before we left he had me throw it all away so I'd have a fighting chance when I got back from rehab.

We waited about five or six hours in the lobby of the treatment center and I was getting sicker by the minute. I finally told him I was going to leave and they got me in immediately. I got a little methadone to taper off with, thank God.

After a week in rehab, my head started to clear. I started to wake up again. It was refreshing to remember what it had been like once to follow my heart and let it guide me toward the light rather than the dark. I realized my downfall had started fifteen months ago, when I made the decision to leave Acton early. I recognized the tendency I had to shut down when merely living became too much to bear.

I was extrapolating on this one night with an older guy who was in there. He must have been sixty or so and a drunk. I'd been talking for a while in this vein and then he looked me straight in the eye and said, "I wish I cared."

I was surprised at first, but when I thought about it I felt a profound sympathy for the man.

"I don't even care about my own life," he said, turning back to his thoughts.

"I understand. I don't either."

After that, I realized I couldn't get through any of this on my own. How many times had I tried and failed? With no other option, I started praying for the lowest common denominator in my complicated equation. I prayed for the desire to stay clean and sober.

Isabela came to see me a few times while I was in treatment. The Los Angeles Kings lost in the playoffs to the Colorado Avalanche after an exciting series over the

Detroit Red Wings and twenty-eight days passed quickly. I got home at about 8:00 a.m. on a weekday and made it to a 9:15 meeting in Studio City.

CHAPTER TWELVE

2001 – 2002

With about three months clean, Mick D. came to visit from Boston. He was sober again and said he missed California. Why wouldn't he? It's beautiful and he'd had a good life there, being useful to other alcoholics and the community. Plus, there were always a ton of girls around and most of them were just lost in Los Angeles.

I had moved my futon bed into Isabela's apartment by that time, for a healthier environment than Dante's. I knew it wouldn't last with her, even if I wanted it to. I was not equipped with the tools and she was becoming more of a responsibility in sobriety. Even after he returned to Boston, Mick kept calling and telling me to move out there and join the Teamsters. He had a two-bedroom apartment on Vinton Street in Southie. I deflected his attempts to sway me for a while, but I always managed to ask him about the one and only Arlene Ryan, how she was doing, and if she was available. I was relentless when I found something to grab onto and I'd already formed a cute fantasy about how everything would be alright if I could just have her.

"Did you tell her I'm out here in California, asking about her?"

"Yeah, yeah. I've told her. She's available and good to go."

I heard the same report so often I began to take it for granted that we were meant to be together and it was just a matter of time. Then, one time I asked him and he said some Puerto Rican guy was hanging around her. The next time I heard from him, Arlene was pregnant.

Well, that takes care of her, I thought. But when I love something, letting go is easier said than done.

Within a couple of weeks I was in Boston, eating chicken parmesan, steak and cheese sandwiches, and steak tips. The food was great and summer was fun in Southie. Winter is a different story. I was grabbing some work with the Teamsters and scalping tickets. In August they brought me up to Willy Derringer's office and I was sworn into the International Brotherhood of Teamsters. In the meantime, there was the usual distraction of girls.

Mick's girlfriend at the time was coming to visit him in Boston and bringing a girlfriend. I was all worked up about that because I heard the friend was a big-time poker player, tall, spunky, and pretty hot. We picked the girls up at the airport and I was excited to see the hot-shot, poker playing Tricia and bring them back to my new apartment. I could see where Tricia might be intimidating, but we were in the sack that night. It was all fun and games but when I was sober I'd get pretty attached so it was hard for me to deal with the fact that she had a serious boyfriend back home, and no intentions of leaving him.

After a two-week stay, she went back to Los Angeles and I was all fucked up, but this time without drugs and alcohol to dull the pain. I didn't know how to process the feelings I was having.

Occasionally over the next year I would run into Arlene here or there and she had baby Sophia with her by that time. I didn't know how to make anything happen with her and I heard that she and Sophia's father were trying to work things out, despite the fact that Arlene's family did everything they could to get rid of him. I was too depressed then to deal with the drama that would surely come from trying to insert myself into a situation like that. To me, she represented another missed opportunity in my life and strengthened my belief that things just never fell into place for me. It was further evidence that I was some sort of mistake that God had made.

I couldn't see that self-pity and ego were dominating my life, but I did manage to stay sober. It took me a while to adjust from big Hollywood and humongous Los Angeles to small, tight-knit South Boston. It was like an institution there. The people seemed abrasive, quick-witted, and confrontational. The fast-pace could be intimidating. I tried to fit in where I could, among different sober groups and had a lot of fun scalping tickets.

Mick and I went out to Salt Lake City for the 2002 Winter Olympics and rented a house for three and a half weeks. We hardly spent any time there because we were always out in the cold, hustling tickets. We led crazy lives but we were making good cash. I was staying clean but it was getting harder and harder. I didn't have much of a spiritual life. I was still bonded to superficial, material things and dedicated the service of my life to these. It was ideals like Arlene that kept me thinking there might be something more for me, but that too was becoming harder and harder to hold on to.

Time went on and in spite of the difficulties I began to

gain some self-confidence and character as I gradually overcame them. I bumped into Arlene one day at a meeting and she told me that Ivan—Sophia's biological father—was coming around again trying to be a sober father and boyfriend. I found myself sitting near him in the meeting and harboring old feelings of jealousy. I found the angst building up inside of me, wanting him to fail. And then I realized what I was doing and pushed aside my judgments and tried to fill my heart with hope for him. It was an amazing thing, opening my heart like that—I actually felt lighter and more optimistic about my own future.

It was a Sunday night, and after the meeting I found myself standing face to face with Arlene amongst the dismantling crowd. Truth be told, I strategically placed myself in her way.

"Do you know how long I've been asking about you?"

She got a big smile on her face and let out a distinctive, flattered laugh.

"You know," I went on, "I've got a Jeep Cherokee that I never use. If you and Sophia need it, you're welcome to use it all day. I take the "T" from Andrew Square to Park Street Station every day for work so the car just sits there on the street."

"Thank you," she said, still smiling, "That's very sweet."

I've never been any good at telling if a girl likes me or not, but I didn't sense her trying to get away or looking disgusted, so I went a little further. I asked her about her brother who lived in West Hollywood and told her if there was ever anything he needed I could find a way to help. She was genuinely appreciative and I was encouraged by the joy of sharing my open and giving heart with her.

We hung out a few more times, with various groups,

and exchanged phone numbers. I spent a lot of time with the sober Southie guys, including Jimmy Mac who was her ex-boyfriend. They'd been together for about seven years before Ivan came along. Jimmy had gangster style, drove a Cadillac and gave off an unapproachable vibe. When we started hanging out, I told him he should be a character actor in Hollywood and he actually pursued that some time later.

"I have to ask man, is there anything still going on between you and Arlene?" I said to Jimmy one night.

"No, no. We're just really close friends."

"Well, I've got her on my heart and I've been thinking...would it cause a strain in our friendship if I asked her out?"

He looked me in the eyes and said, "No. You've got my word. But I really appreciate the respect, man."

It was the right thing to do. In my short time in Boston I'd learned so much from the people there. They all had class. And all my life it had been hard for me to deal with having hurt someone.

After that, Jimmy Mac was supportive of my mission and even found ways for Arlene and I to cross paths more. A week later, Arlene and I went on our first date. I took her to the Wang Theater to see "Rent." It was great and we both had a lot of fun.

Then, the next night, I hung out with Mick and out of nowhere he got obsessed with the idea of using dope.

The cycle began again. I tried to find reasons not to use but the more time I spent thinking about it the more I felt I had the mental defenses in place to handle it. Besides, shouldn't I just do it and stop obsessing? So I snorted some heroin. How could I not? Some things had changed, but my mind was still the same warped tool that caused me to falter many times before. So there I was, high off my ass and going to meet up with Arlene. The worst part had to be hiding what I'd done from the girl I was crazy about. But the thing about dope addicts is that we have a very keen sense for when someone around us is using. We talked for about a minute and a half before Arlene said, "You sound jammed."

"What?"

"You are so high right now!"

I denied it and said I had to get going, but she knew. Arlene had been addicted to heroin when she was younger and had been clean since she was nineteen. In Southie, heroin and pills were wildly popular and pretty accessible compared to L.A. Two days later we met again and I sounded better without that groggy heroin voice. But she persisted. Finally, she got a confession out of me.

"Well, I have a confession too," she said, "I want to use."

This terrified me more than her finding out about my relapse.

"No way! No," I said.

This was Arlene Ryan, with nine and a half years clean and sober. In a small neighborhood like Southie, where community is more of a clan, I would be treated like a pariah if anyone found out that I had a hand in Arlene's relapse. Still, she kept pushing and telling me that she had already broke out using her dad's Percocet. My weak mind gave in.

I was scared to death of how people would react if they found out what we were doing. We had booked a flight for Los Angeles so we could spend Thanksgiving there and we were taking Sophia with us. We were scheduled to leave within a week of relapsing. What a fucking mess. It was cold in Boston. Arlene's family knew we were up to no good and they were panicking about two-year-old Sophia's safety. If they had ousted Ivan from the family, it was nothing to what they were prepared to do to me.

Before I slid back to heroin, I felt for the first time in my life like things were working out. Instead of getting her pregnant and being forced into something, I had a chance to spend time with Arlene and Sophia and be respectable. I had begun to think maybe I could do this. Maybe I could be a family man. And there we were getting high.

The night before our flight we stayed up all night shooting dope. A few months before that, when I was still clean, I was walking home from Andrew Station and saw a girl who lived four doors down from me out on her front stoop with a nod so heavy it looked like her head weighed a hundred pounds. My first thought was that I wanted to boot her as hard as I could for being so high she couldn't even lift her head. But then I felt bad, realizing that she probably had no other way to get through a day on her own. She must have been living with so much hurt, fear, and remorse. I actually pitied her.

Arlene and I took turns going into the bathrooms at Logan Airport to shoot up. We got to LAX and borrowed my sister's van. Before the sun went down we were down at the Nickel, the popular name for 5th Street, in downtown L.A., to cop dope. Still, there was that part of me that understood the severity of what I'd done. Part of me still couldn't believe that two weeks ago I was one-and-a-half years clean and now I was telling Arlene Ryan and little

Sophia to sit tight while I grabbed some heroin. I stuck out like a sore thumb in that part of town and that filled me with fear. I imagined getting pinched while they were sitting there, waiting for me while it got dark in downtown Los Angeles. Arlene didn't even have a driver's license and never had. She was a Boston city girl—a fish out of water in monstrous L.A. What was I doing?

I dirtied my appearance up and ran the gauntlet. I was still looking too clean, and didn't have heavy track marks so all the street dealers I went to thought I was a cop. I started getting angry and I think they finally sensed my real desperation. That was something they recognized. I managed to get black and white—a mix of heroin and coke—and had to face the challenge of getting back to the car with so much anxiety and dope on me. An undercover can pounce on you any second and I had to remind myself to walk slow and wander a little, carrying myself like I had no home.

But I did have a home, didn't I? I made it back to the minivan feeling like a gazelle that just snuck through a fucking herd of cheetahs. From there we had to screw around with rush-hour traffic on the 101 freeway just to get to a less conspicuous spot. We finally made it a few exits away, out of the thick of it. Sophia was coming unglued after being in a car seat and on an airplane all day. Arlene and I tied off and both fixed in the van and only hoped Sophia didn't see or know the extent of what we'd done.

CHAPTER THIRTEEN

February 2003 - February 14, 2004

When we got back to Boston, I knew I was in over my head. South Boston was, as I mentioned, a tight-knit community. One of the only good things that came with this was that it offered a sort of built-in accountability. When Micky checked into Long Island Detox after the New Year, it gave me an incentive to follow.

Arlene and I both returned from our trip to Los Angeles knowing that we had to get our acts together. It was a fun trip, a chance to get away, but I'd been getting away for so long in my mind that I could hardly remember what it felt like to be grounded to something solid. Arlene and Sophia were solid. Arlene's resolve to get clean on her own—and the strength she demonstrated in doing so—were just another push in the right direction.

I was admitted to Long Island Detox two days after Mick, and Alex joined us two days later, followed by our buddy Steven two days after that. That was the way things were done in Southie, where everyone knew everything about you. Being in detox for twenty-one days with some of my closest friends was a recipe for disaster. We all had cell phones with us even though we weren't supposed to and we got into a fair bit of harmless trouble, but it was healing in its own way. Everyone was funny in Long Island, but we were sick, too. And it was dreary as hell. That part of the world was dying for spring to arrive.

I knew that when I got out of there I had to do something more. Everything I built always crumbled and I was just a jackass with a sledgehammer. I always ended up right back where I started and I knew I needed a major adjustment. I needed to get my head straight if I wanted anything I ever did to last. I couldn't just rip through Arlene and Sophia's life leaving a path of pain behind me. I had to learn to put down the tools of my own destruction. I had to either get well or get back to dying, but to determine what I was destined for I had to go back to the source. California was calling to me.

Alex and I got out of Long Island on the same day and I'm glad for the time we had together now. We got on the subway and parted ways at our stop. He said he was going to get some pills so he could sell them. It was one of the last times I saw him. A couple of years later he was back on cocaine and fresh out of prison. He ran into the lobby of the Four Seasons in Boston where he died at about 4:00 a.m. on a Sunday morning. He was reportedly choked out by the security guards. Like most drug-related deaths, I never really knew what happened.

I left three days after I got out of detox. I went to a couple of meetings and made the rounds to all of my friends, still sweating a little, but healthy enough to see everyone and tell them face-to-face that I was leaving. They all seemed to understand, for the most part, or said they did. Arlene was a different story. She sent Sophia from the room and sat in front of me with tears on her cheeks and so many unanswered questions in her voice. Really, it all came down to just one question: "How long will you be gone?"

"I don't know," I answered. "Sixty days, ninety...I really don't know. You can come if you want—move out there for the time being."

"I can't. You know I can't, not without knowing..." she said.

Her face spoke the truth that neither of us wanted to face. I didn't know when I'd be coming back, or if I would. I just knew I had to start and the rest would be determined by how strong I was; how willing and ready for a life-altering change. Arlene didn't want to hear this. She just said, "I hope you take the time to really find what it is you're looking for." When we said good-bye at last, her eyes were dry.

I made a few phone calls to guys who were involved in recovery back in L.A. to make sure I had a place to stay when I got there. Jerry and Miles were the first people I contacted and they had room for me in the three-bedroom house they were renting by themselves. From there it was just a matter of crossing the distance to a new way of life.

It took me five days to cross the country. I stopped where I wanted and attended meetings in whatever town I was in. I saw the Grand Canyon for the first time in my life and paced myself. It was a new and different way of living in the moment and I stared out at the great abyss of towering canyon walls beneath me and felt for the first time that perspective is something that demands more respect. I'd been at the bottom for so long, it felt like a miracle to see things from a different point of view.

From Arizona it was just a matter of a day before I was driving into the black and blue skyline of Los Angeles. I returned with mixed feelings. What would my life be from here? What would I make of this opportunity, or what would it make of me? Along the way it had felt like there were so many bends and turns in the path, but looking back it seemed like all but a straight line. I'd never diverged. I'd always done the same thing in the same way. I tried to see L.A. in a new light but it scared me that I couldn't. So I moved forward with my eyes cast backward on the past.

I went to meetings and reconnected with Miles and Jerry. Hours passed and I could not differentiate one from the other. In meetings I always felt like I was on the verge of something great. I felt like the veil to some great secret of life was being peeled away slowly and I wanted nothing more than to rip and claw at it, peeling back the surface to get at the truth that had eluded me for so long. But if there was one thing I'd learned from my numerous sponsors over the years, it was that I had to pace myself; take things day by day, moment by moment.

After a meeting one night, I set out to walk home since the night was warm and carried with it the promise of an early spring. While I walked I reflected on the past, wondering where I went wrong but recognizing that there was a common denominator. *What is wrong with me?* I asked myself. And then I realized that was it. I was always blaming myself, hating myself, abusing myself. How could I love someone else, or be worthy of love, if I couldn't even love myself?

Two months turned into four and I talked to Arlene on the phone once in a while. She'd asked me a few times when I thought I might be coming back but my answer was always the same. I didn't know. After a while she stopped asking and I could feel the subtle shift in her attitude. She was slowly withdrawing her belief in my eventual return. It made me sad, but I didn't blame her and I was even a little relieved to know that she didn't have unreasonable expectations of me. I didn't know what to expect one day to the next, so I couldn't ask her to. Instead, I tried to get over her.

Miles ran into an old girlfriend and started things up again with her. I turned to whoever I was using and in the end we'd sit around smoking cigarettes, drinking coffee, and sorting out the drama of our lives. Listening to Miles lament over difficulties with his girlfriend, I thought how strange it was that he didn't seem to remember the reason he'd decided not to be with her in the first place. But wasn't I doing the same thing? I'd fallen into the same old cycle of replacing one drug with another; heroin with sex. It was all just a Band-Aid to mask the gaping wound.

I left Boston in March and by June I was calling Arlene less and less. In one of our conversations she told me she'd gone on a few dates with a guy. It really got to me to know that she was moving on but I couldn't just tell her to go to hell. I couldn't quite be done with her. Still, I didn't tell her it upset me, and I didn't sell her some false promise of my return. I hung up the phone and lived hour by hour until I could set out walking to the next meeting.

It was strange, but by doing the right thing I began to understand where I had gone wrong for so long. I always allowed my own will to take over, serving only myself, instead of letting a greater will guide me into usefulness to others. It was maybe the first time that I really understood the importance of a higher power in my life. I'd never really given recovery a chance because I'd never really given myself over to it.

Months later I was working as an art director and set designer for Discovery and the History Channel. It was a glamorous job and I was making good money. But what did I really have to show for it? Jimmy Mac had moved out from Southie and was getting his start in Hollywood, and the sight of him reminded me of everything I'd never have if I didn't have Arlene. I was doing a decent job of letting God be the light in my life and I was hanging out in grace, but I wasn't really being the kind of change that I wanted to see in my life.

After wrestling with the idea for a few weeks, talking with Arlene, and praying for guidance, I decided that I was going to give love the best shot I'd ever given it. I put in my notice, finished my last two weeks of work and cut my ties, for the last time, with Los Angeles. The day after Christmas I loaded up my faithful Jeep Cherokee and hit the I-10 freeway heading east. Watching the city fade away behind me was like leaving a woman who'd been a good lover but a bad friend.

Incidentally, it was the last time I would ever see Miles or Jerry alive. Jerry died on the way to a meeting on his motorcycle some years later and Miles overdosed on cocaine. It seemed at times that there were so many lost souls in my past.

The first day of my travels, I made it to Flagstaff, Arizona. It was cold in the desert and I slept in my car, loaded down with blankets, but I still woke at 3:30 in the morning feeling like an icicle. I ran the engine and heat for another hour of broken sleep. Was I crazy? I had just driven this same road in the opposite direction at the end of last winter. Now here I was, nine months clean and sober, with no guarantee that I could make it work and that I wouldn't continue to travel the same broken roads without any end in sight.

I thought of little Sophia, who was three and a half now, and wondered if she would accept me back into her life. One day passed to another as the thoughts reeled. I drove through the Appalachian Mountains and upstate New York with doubt and excitement swirling in my head like always. But mostly I felt like I was doing the right thing by giving God a chance to work in my life.

I finally pulled up to 17 M Street and walked up to the second floor of the three-story apartment building with unprecedented resolve. I took a few deep breaths before I knocked, trying to be present and realize what I was committing to. I'd never had a problem opening my heart, but never had I done it with such conviction. I waited a moment before I heard her footsteps and Arlene opened the door with a smile that offered everything and accepted me in.

Arlene and I had already talked a lot about how to tell her parents and Sophia about our renewed relationship. Sophia warmed up to me quickly again, but it was a slow process to earn the respect of Arlene's family. With them, I often felt like I was trying to nuzzle up to a grizzly bear that's nice enough, but still a wild animal. I went back to work with the Teamsters, went to meetings, and focused on honoring my responsibilities and offering myself in a useful capacity. Gradually, Arlene's family recognized that I was trying to do the right thing and that I was sincere and they warmed to me.

Everyone knew that I was back in Boston to marry Arlene, but the matter of asking her was still unresolved. Valentine's Day was three weeks away and I was thinking in that direction. I decided to see about an engagement ring first. My good friend Alex was a well-known jewel thief and I entertained the thought of going to him for a moment. But I really didn't want to give Arlene a stolen ring, convinced that it would curse our marriage. Instead, I was referred to Keith Alpine, a friend and fellow Teamster. He was always working with antiques and suggested that I buy an antique diamond ring.

"Think about it," he reasoned, "A hundred years ago stuff was a lot more quality."

The demand for antique jewelry wasn't great so the market was low, and I had Keith's knowledge behind me. We went to an antique store and I quickly saw that he was right. The old gems seemed flawless and completely original. I picked out a really cool platinum ring with a small diamond. The beautiful cut and setting made it shine and seem bigger than it actually was. I got it for a good price and was pleased with the first step in my plan. Now, with the ring in hand, the rest was slowly falling into place.

The day before Valentine's Day, I came home from work and told Arlene I had a surprise for her. She looked at me skeptically, but with an indulgent smile.

"I want you and Sophia to pack your bags. I'm driving us all to New York City for Valentine's Day."

She started to ask about the money, but I stopped her with a kiss and told her I wouldn't answer any questions. I wanted to show her a good time without letting her worry about anything. We had a reservation at the Hotel Pennsylvania, across from Madison Square Garden. It was

163

a long drive getting there and a tough night in the hotel. Sophia, who we called Little Pipi, was being a handful and really spoiling my idea of a romantic, sex-filled night. I wished there was a way to tranquilize her, but I also admired her energy. She had a lot of it!

We woke up on Valentine's Day and I gave both of my beautiful girls a card, a little stuffed animal, and some chocolates. I apologized for not being able to do more and hoped they weren't disappointed, but Arlene was grateful and when she looked out the hotel window as if the whole world was ours for the taking, I was convincingly reminded that she was the woman for me. After a day in the city, we went back to the hotel room to gather a few additional articles of clothing, and for me to slip the engagement ring into my pocket. Then we headed down to Rockefeller Center for an evening of ice skating.

The ring might as well have been a kilo of coke that I was smuggling for how nervous I was. I turned it over and over in my pocket. We got into the rink and skated for a while. I was clowning around and taking turns twirling Sophia and Arlene around. They were both rosy-cheeked from the cold and from laughing. Then, as if I suddenly remembered, I said, "I forgot, I have one more gift for you both."

"Oh no," Arlene said, laughing over whatever goofy stunt she thought I might pull next.

"Check this out."

I skated away from them, then turned around and skated back, sliding at the last moment onto one knee and holding the ring out.

"Will you marry me?"

Arlene blushed and I looked up into those gorgeous, smiling Irish eyes. She was nodding her head and people were starting to notice what was happening. They broke out in applause as I stood and took a bow.

"She said yes!" I called and the applause grew louder.

Say what you want, but New Yorkers are classy people. And I was the luckiest guy in the world.

Afterward, back in the hotel room, I pulled out a little ring that I'd purchased for Sophia and sat her on my lap. I asked her if she would marry me, too. She giggled and nodded and showed the ring off to Arlene who was looking at me like I had never been looked at by a woman. She hugged us both and told me how happy she was. It was a beautiful moment and one that I knew had to be done. I wasn't just marrying Arlene, I was marrying her daughter. And if I had learned one thing through my mistakes, it was that we either have to do things all the way, or not at all.

On our way back home, it was clear something was wrong. The Jeep started making a clunking noise and finally died on the side of the road near Providence, Rhode Island. A look under the hood told me the transfer case had gone out and we wouldn't be getting it running any time soon. But it didn't faze us much. I had my two best girls and together we had the world. We caught a bus to South Station and Sophia fell asleep between us on the long ride. I looked at Arlene over her sleeping head and realized that I'd traded one kind of thrill for another. It was just another adventurous, sober Saturday night.

CHAPTER FOURTEEN

2004 - 2012

All of my family, with the exception of Tina—my oldest sister—were able to come out to Boston for the wedding. My parents were supportive of my decision to marry Arlene. They had met her and Sophia with open arms. It didn't even seem to bother them that I wasn't marrying a Mormon girl and towing the line. Or that Arlene was newly pregnant with my child when we tied the knot. I think they were grateful that I'd spent the last several years independent from them and that I was open to taking on responsibility. So, I was happy to have them there.

The wedding was held on June 19, 2004, in Quincy, Massachusetts, which was the town just to the south of South Boston. We initially wanted a beach wedding because we envisioned something light and lovely. That's one of the things I adored about Arlene—she was artsy and bohemian and happy living a simple life, not asking for much. She could slip on any old dress and look like a supermodel. Slowly, however, our idyllic wedding morphed into something slightly more grandiose, but the gazebo setting where we said our vows was perfect in the end. The gazebo sat over the water at the Adam's Inn, where I'd stayed a few times when smuggling drugs. It was an unfortunate connection I tried to push out of my mind that day.

There were 120 guests in attendance, including Arlene's large family, many of our Boston friends, the Teamster boss, my closest coworkers, and my sponsor. Sophia and my nephew Ethan were the ring-bearers. It was our day, our time, and life positively shone with promise. After the ceremony, we went to Bermuda for our honeymoon, just Arlene and me. And in all the beautiful days that followed, I found one thing to be most extraordinary: I didn't necessarily plan any of this— Valentine's Day, becoming a father, celebrating one year of sobriety—I couldn't have. I wasn't that good on my own. But I found that everything was better when I just showed up and enacted God's plan for my life.

Surprisingly, marriage required little adjustment. Arlene and Sophia and I had been living together before, but we now shared an added bond between us. Our life consisted of living in Arlene's apartment, working, going to meetings, and being heavy into recovery. Prior to getting married we had tried two different Christian churches, feeling our way through the messages they each gave and feeling unsatisfied by both. Arlene had been raised in an established and tight-knit Catholic family but I admired her open-mindedness to new religions. She wanted something that spoke to her. As someone who had always lead with my heart, this aspect of her character jived really well with mine.

Eventually, we were led to the Presbyterian Church on Vinton Street where I had first seen Arlene and where Reverend Burns delivered the Sunday sermon. Whereas the Christian ministers had refused to marry us because we were living in sin, Reverend Burns accepted us and of course I loved him because he withheld judgment.

At the same time, the Teamsters union was in the hot seat and guys were getting called down left and right for racketeering. It was a tough time but I learned a lot about corruption and politics, which is one of the casualties of being present in life. Facing reality is never easy to get used to.

And then came reality of a different kind. In December, 2004, our daughter Julia was born. It was the coolest, scariest moment of my life up to that point and when it came down to the raw emotion of her birth, I could not imagine not being wholly present for it. It was freezing outside and we were up all night. I stayed by Arlene's side, coaching her and trying to be whatever she needed. Then, after hours of labor, Julia came into the world and my eyes welled with tears when I saw her for the first time. I saw and felt God in that moment and I was humbled. I couldn't believe that any of it was real but I wanted to live in that moment, that feeling, forever.

As time went by and we were hauling a baby around and facing daily life, it began to dawn on me that Julia was actually mine and that I had actually married the woman of my dreams and somehow found my way to a perfect life. Not to say it wasn't without its challenges. To a recovering drug addict and alcoholic, even the most trivial struggles seem monumental. My only hope was to take one day at a time, being thankful for what I had and never losing sight of how I got there.

In the spring, we went to California on vacation and stayed with my brother Tim in Sacramento. He was still an avid Mormon and on Sunday morning I came to the awkward realization that we either had to go with him and his family to church or spend three hours alone at their house. Arlene gave me a nudge and nodded, so I told Tim that we would be joining them for the morning service.

When we got there, Sophia went to Primary with Tim's children and Arlene went with them. I sat through the entire three hours trying to push away the vague memories of the past and trying to appear as happy and non-conflicted as everyone around me. It was an exercise in futility and I just ended up feeling like an inadequate teenager among so many clean and shining people. Thank God I only had to do it the one time.

Afterward, Arlene and Sophia and I were standing on the broad sidewalk in front of the church while Tim and his family chatted with friends.

"I really liked that church," Arlene said, "I couldn't believe how clearly they explained the gospel to the little kids. It was amazing."

"Slow down, there," I chuckled, "You don't want to go getting involved with this group. It'll ruin all our fun." I was trying to be playful about it, but inside I felt a sort of dread.

When we were on our way back to Weymouth, Arlene brought it up again.

"I'd really like to try going to an LDS church near us. Do you think it would be the same?"

"It will be exactly the same. They're very consistent."

She was quiet for a moment.

"I know it's not what you would choose, Tommy, but I really can't explain how much it affected me, being there. I'd like to at least give it a shot."

As it turned out, we didn't go right away. Life was busy and I, of course, avoided bringing up the subject. I worked hard and we were making a good living for our family of four. Before long, we found an apartment to rent in a town south of Quincy, called Weymouth. Our first lease fell through just before we were getting ready to move in, so we had to scramble to find an apartment in another complex. That's where we met Roger and Michelle Dillard.

As soon as we moved in, the Dillards brought over some treats and introduced themselves as our neighbors. When they left, I told Arlene, "I bet they're Mormons."

They were. When they invited us over for dinner not long after, Arlene was eager to learn if there was an LDS church nearby. The Dillards told us about the Hingham ward and said they would love to see us there sometime. By way of explanation, I told them we had just visited my brother in Sacramento and attended the LDS church with them there.

"We knew a Womeldorf who used to live in Braintree, about ten years ago," Roger said.

After further questioning, we discovered that it was Tim. Roger had attended the same church as Tim and Roger and his sister had even babysat Tim's oldest daughter on occasion. To Arlene this was a sign that everything up to this point had happened for a reason.

The following Sunday, we were sitting in church next to Roger and Michelle. Arlene was obviously having a beautiful experience, so I did my best to enjoy myself by engaging the people around me in conversation. We did meet some great people that day and in the following months. I particularly enjoyed Roger's parents who were converted hippies and shared an open and loving attitude. Just as I had in every other church we'd attended, I got into fellowship and tried to get as much out of religion as it had to offer, but it was clear to me that I didn't feel the connection that others shared with the Church. I was invited to talk about these feelings with the bishop and I did. He tried to ameliorate my concerns and when it came down to it I couldn't specifically say what it was about the Church that I deplored, because I wasn't ready to examine where those deep-seated feelings came from. So when Arlene was baptized into the church in 2005, it was me who performed the baptism and I was ready to give the Mormon religion what I could.

Moving to Weymouth had been a big step for Arlene. For the most part, her whole family lived within the same neighborhood in Southie, and always had. But we were destined to always move to the beat of our own drum and no one had been too surprised by that move. The real shock came a year later when we made the decision to move out of Massachusetts altogether. With all the drama that had been going on in our local union, many of the guys were considering what they would do if things fell apart. One of the guys told me that if things went south he was going to move to Phoenix, Arizona. There was affordable housing and plenty of work to be had in the desert.

I kicked the idea around for a while and before long I had a yearning to move. We had our choices narrowed down to Las Vegas, Phoenix, or Sacramento, because there was growth in all of these places. Boston was an old city, but elsewhere in the world things were happening for the first time. It seemed fitting that our new life should have a new backdrop. Several opportunities popped up in Arizona, so we decided on Phoenix and started packing for the move.

The change was hardest on Arlene. Leaving Boston behind was like severing the umbilical cord that still tied her to her family. Seeing how stoically she handled it not only made me admire her more but also gave me some insight into how much faith she had in me; in us. I filed for unemployment in Massachusetts, which had the highest cost of living in the U.S. and this supported us while we got on our feet in Arizona, where the cost of living was among the lowest.

We found a new ward to belong to and, in 2007, our family was sealed in the Mesa Arizona Temple. We continued to attend church and practice our faith. I was piecing together work where I could find it and had a few leads. We made friends quickly and not long after we moved, Sophia was invited to a birthday party and Arlene went with her. When she came home, Arlene was even more excited than Sophia.

"You'll never guess," she said, "I met a husband and wife who are remodeling their house and we got to talking. They said they were looking for a carpenter to help finish the work on the house. She's a realtor and he's in business so they don't have a lot of time for it themselves. I told them you have tons of experience in construction and they want to meet with you. Isn't that great?"

"Well, it would be, if I had any tools."

"That's the thing—the have all the tools you'd need for the job, and materials too. You just have to show up and get the work done."

As it turned out, they were also willing to pay cash, and regularly. So, I began spending my days in their garage, putting together some great projects. I added a second story to their house and did a lot of custom work. And all the while I kept thinking how I could turn that one-time gig into something more. But the best thing that came from the association was that the wife told me, when I had finished with the job, that if we were ever in the market for a house, she could get us a great deal.

After that, one remodeling job turned into another and I began building up and running my own carpentry business. However, Arlene and I both couldn't get over the dream of owning our own home. When we went back to visit our realtor friend, she told us that there was no reason why we couldn't qualify for a loan, as long as we had paystubs to prove my income. Well, that put a hiccup in our plans. I was earning mostly cash, paid under the table, for the work I'd been taking on. I would have to get some documented earnings if I wanted to keep our dream alive.

I began sniffing around at a job that one of my buddies had told me about. It was another union job, setting up for trade shows in the greater Phoenix area. I went in for an interview and soon had the job. With the most important box checked, Arlene and I didn't want to wait around for a requisite number of years before we could document enough earnings to satisfy a mortgage company. So we decided to proceed with securing a loan, put out what we had, and told them to call Mick Denali to confirm that I had worked at my current place of employment for over two years. It wasn't entirely a lie. I had shifted companies, but had consistently and loyally worked for the union for much more than that amount of time. In the long run, I would see how ill-advised that move was.

In our quest for God, or religion, or whatever guides us, we are never perfect. Life is a process of striving and learning. I got it wrong. More than once I got it wrong. The darkness was still there, hovering on the periphery like a cataract that would never go away. I sought the light, as we all do, but sometimes it was only to balance the darkness.

We moved into the house we bought and it was clean and new; a blank slate. I was on top of the world, a proven provider for my family and a basically happy guy. We attended church regularly and aside from inexplicable bouts of anxiety and anger on Sunday morning—which I didn't care to explore the meaning of—all was well. Maybe I was flying too close to the sun. We made friends in our neighborhood and I took a particular liking to Steve. He was a family man, like myself, and seemed to have his shit together. Arlene and I continued to attend recovery meetings and everything was copacetic and easy and pretty much on auto-pilot. These are the times when we lose touch. We forget the desperation with which we should be seeking.

After a year, the market started to drop and there was talk of a recession. I didn't see the need to panic. When we found out Arlene was pregnant again it was another cause to celebrate our good fortune. I added another task to the laundry list prayer I handed up to God each morning at 5 a.m.: *Please watch over Arlene and the kids and the baby, and help me to do good at work and pay the bills. Help me to be a good husband and dad. And please watch over our house and protect our stuff...*

There wasn't a lot going on there besides a recitation of my wants, along with a few needs.

Then, one sunny day I came home from work to find our street swarming with police cars, fire trucks and ambulances. My heart jumped in my throat but it was immediately clear that they weren't near our house, but further down the street. The action was centered around Steve's house and officers came and went through the front door. I hurried inside and found Arlene sitting with the girls and reading them a book. She handed Sophia the book to finish reading to her sister and took my arm to pull me out of the room.

"I was trying to distract them. They were scared when they heard the sirens and saw all of the police cars. I don't know how to tell them…"

"What happened?"

Arlene's eyes were red.

"It's Steve. He killed himself. I just can't believe it, he seemed so—like everything was alright."

The words hit me like a brick wall. All right. Everything was all right.

The news of Steve's death took a toll on me that I hadn't expected. How was it that one moment I could be sailing along under bright skies and then suddenly I was flailing about in a turbulent sea? The answer was self-evident. Everything hadn't been all right. Sure, things were great on the surface, but that's just what it was: *superficial*. I had been falling into the same materialistic trap. Rather than actively pursuing the influences of God, I had allowed myself to linger in the effects of his grace; allowed myself to believe that's all there was.

I didn't know how to right the sinking ship. I looked at Arlene, her belly bulging with our unborn daughter, and I looked at Sophia and Julia, both growing more beautiful each day, and realized despairingly that they could offer no salvation. I found myself thinking of Steve often, drawn to whatever dark impulses had caused him to end his own life. I had to tell myself to stop, but the thoughts were always there. If he had succumbed to the darkness, how on earth could someone like me escape it? I was reminded that life is just a series of horrors interrupted by a few moments of bliss. I longed for a drink.

I wanted to forget the black thoughts and the bottle seemed the only tool within my reach. I craved the instant medication that alcohol offered. After seven years of sobriety, I was in a hopeless place. Drinking, drugs, suicide...they were all right around the corner, waiting for me. All I had to do was turn my head. I went to meetings trying to find one thing to grasp onto like a lifeline. Everyone there was full of easy grace and so many were thankful for a new job or a minor victory. I suddenly saw the banality of such things in the state I was in and knew that I needed to seek answers elsewhere.

I talked to Arlene a little about my struggles and we decided that I should try a men's group. I found one nearby and attended my first meeting. I recognized immediately that the guys were a bit more revealing and honest here than in the co-ed meetings. I started attending regularly. Most of the guys were artists and I liked the vibe I got from them. They were laid-back and nonjudgmental. In the group of five to nine guys each week, one in particular stood out to me.

Les blew my mind pretty quickly. It didn't happen often, but I was open to it and somehow he spoke to whatever was yearning within me. I remembered seeing him a time or two at the co-ed meetings and hearing him share then. I remembered that he'd gotten a little choked up when he did. Of course I dismissed him as soft back then, but only because I hadn't been ready to hear his message.

He opened one night by saying, "Unconditional Love..."

My ears perked up.

"Ever had it? No. I see you shaking your heads, smiling. But you want to know the truth? You have. You *do*. But it's not out there in the perfect job or the perfect woman or the perfect life. It's not at the bottom of a bottle, or the peak of a high either. It's inside each of us and it has been since the day we were born. We all have unconditional love, right here inside of us. What you've come searching for, you've come searching with..."

See? Totally blown away. I dissected this idea over the next few days, but I found that it raised more questions than answers. The following week we did a five minute meditation at the beginning of the meeting and, afterward, as everyone else filtered out to the parking lot, I stayed behind until it was just Les and I. He was completely cool when I told him, point blank, that I just wanted to hear more. He really started to blow my mind then.

"I can see that you want answers. You're no different than the rest of us. We are all seekers, looking for a connection to something greater than ourselves. Sometimes we find something similar in alcohol or heroin, but it's inauthentic. The real thing, though, really does exist. Somewhere along the way I was touched by God and I'll tell you, Tommy, nothing less will ever do. It was the real thing—*is* the real thing. That's what you have to understand, God is always with us, always in us. We just have all these issues, wants, judgments, and shit covering it up. We go wrong in our search when we're held back by our attachments and the price tag of religion. There are expectations placed on us at every turn. For instance, we learn that it's wrong to say bad words, but what are bad words? What makes them bad? It's just a label we've given to something completely innocuous. These are the types of judgments and attachments that cloud our minds. They prevent us from seeing what's real."

I listened in rapt attention. It was so simple, what he said, but it was the way he demonstrated such a desperate need for these connections that I could relate to.

"You're a father, so let me ask you...do you remember when your first child was born and you had that feeling of utterly selfless bliss? Do you remember looking at your wife in awe and seeing her as nothing more than a beautiful woman who gave life to your child? When you look at your children, do you see their pure innocence? *That's* where we need to live. We need to find a home right there in the absence of motive, the absence of filters. That's where unconditional love is. Deep down in every man, woman, and child there is a fundamental knowledge of God. It's not up to us to decide who or what God is, it's up to us to connect with that *place* where God resides.

"Tommy," Les said, "I have a recording in my car that I'd like to share with you. I want you to take it home with you and listen to it. You might get more out of it than I have to offer."

"I doubt that. I'm afraid you may be changing my life with this stuff, Les. It feels like the deepest thing I've ever learned but it's so damn simple."

We stepped out into the cool night air.

"Of course it is. The ego resists what's simple. We try to complicate everything. We use trouble as something to hide behind. We do this because we don't want to deal with things, but the only real way to let go of our problems is to let them out. The more we hold onto old wounds and pain, the more they color our perception of reality. The path to

God is a subtraction process. It's about removing these negative influences from your life, not about adding God into the mix."

We reached his car then and I was just dumbfounded. I felt suddenly alive and motivated and inspired. Of course, it couldn't all be as easy as that to put into practice, but to know that enlightenment was achievable, that people like me had found it before, well that was the very definition of hope that I needed in that moment.

Les put the key in the ignition to start the car so he could extract the CD from its player. The engine wheezed but wouldn't turn over. He tried a few more times to no effect. He looked up at me and smiled.

"You'd think I'd planned this, now, wouldn't you?"

I laughed because it certainly did seem ironic in the face of what we'd been discussing. I told him to pop the hood and we peered under it together.

"It's gotta be the battery," I said. "I've got some jumper cables in my car."

We ended up jumping his car and I gladly told him to keep the cables because I had an extra pair in the garage at home. I felt great about it because of how much he had helped me. It was a reminder of how many opportunities we really have to learn and thrive in life, if only we are open and willing to recognize them.

I parted from Les knowing that I still had much to learn from him, and eager for our next meeting. When I was on the road, I called Arlene.

"I'm sorry I'm late," I said, "I was just experiencing some heavy shit. Arlene, you wouldn't believe it. I met this guy and he...I swear he fucking changed everything I ever thought I knew."

"It must have been good. I can hear it in your voice."

"Well, I promise I'm not on acid, even though I feel like I am."

She laughed, totally understanding.

"Hurry home, then. I can't wait to hear about it."

That night we put the girls to bed and went to sit on the patio to talk about my experience with Les. I told her everything he'd said and she listened, absorbing it all as I had. When I finished, we both didn't know what to say. Life is a series of discoveries. I looked up to my left and there was a full moon looking back at me and tears clouded my vision. I realized then that I'd been protected. I'd almost forgotten that it was just that morning when I'd thrown up the most desperate and sincere prayer I'd uttered in a long time.

God," I had whispered, on my knees after another long and restless night, "Please, God. If you do exist you have to show yourself to me. Please...give me something. I'm all done here and you know that. I've got no way over this and I know you can see that. Please help me. I can't let Arlene and the girls watch me go down in a big way, but it's coming and I need you."

Now, in the moonlight with Arlene I could see that my prayer had been answered. I'd never had any problem yelling at God or telling him just what I was feeling. But I often felt guilty over all the times I'd cursed the shit out of him in hard times or fits of rage. I'd been sure for so long that he didn't care about me. I thought he'd abandoned me, but he'd been there all along, right there inside of me where I was too afraid to look; God was in me like the ocean is in a wave.

Fiona was born and was followed by our fourth daughter, Lola, in the summer of 2009. Meanwhile, the market continued to dive and I maintained my fearsome commitment to learning a new way of life with the help of Les, who was now my sponsor. Still, in 2012, we lost our house to foreclosure and it was a hard knock. I learned to use a new perspective to fight the old and all-to-familiar feelings of failure and dejection.

We found a house to rent a few miles away. We put the girls in school and set out to reestablish some stability, both financially and mentally. We soon found out that there was a huge Mormon population in Gilbert and lo and behold we found ourselves right in the mix of a new ward. The one thing that did not change was that I continued to have bouts of stress-induced anger prior to attending church on Sundays. I began to realize, however, that the more I grew in my understanding of God's role in my life, the more detached I grew from the Church.

I mentioned this to Les one night after another meeting.

"Tommy, you've come clean with me. I think it's time you come clean with yourself."

CHAPTER FIFTEEN

2012-2013

I learned a lot from Les. He was older than me by maybe eight years and grew up a Christian in South Dakota. Religion didn't have the same effects on his sister, growing up right alongside him, but it damaged Les somehow. He viewed it as a cult that he just didn't fit into. So it was strange to hear him talk about God. He had this clear idea that God is just the name we give to unconditional love. Of course, religion interprets God this way, but it also strives to make God marketable. The way Les described God made the idea simple and beautiful, exactly as it is meant to be.

Les taught me the real concept of unconditional love. He taught me to wipe my "belief slate" clean and live in the light of pure love. This is the love that comes with no conditions, attachments, or expectations. It is so hard to find in our lives when our conscious minds are laden with judgment. We live this way without even realizing there's a purer state of being that's available to us. But as soon as I understood this, it was easy to see how deluded I'd been for most of my life. I had been faced with the added challenge—which I preferred to consider a blessing—of having four daughters to raise. That would put a fair amount of pressure on anyone, let alone an older father with a background of instability. Looking at Sophia, Julia, Fiona, and Lola, I realized that I never planted myself solidly anywhere because I was so afraid of being a disappointment. But now I realized that I couldn't be a disappointment, as long as I showed up and gave every moment my best shot. I learned to banish guilt and doubt and self-loathing. Those are just the trappings of a life lived in constant judgment of ourselves and those around us.

When we lost our first house, the home we rented in Gilbert was owned by a Mormon couple. They were wealthy and ran a big law firm in Mesa, Arizona. About a year or so into our lease, we fell into some tough times financially and had trouble paying our rent. We contacted them and told them the situation. Our payments were going to be late for a few months. Their suggestion was that we solicit the bishop of our ward for assistance in meeting our financial obligations. Talk about a hard pill to swallow. Arlene and I talked about it for a long time. It was demoralizing to have to ask this corporation for crumbs to survive when we knew how miserly they could be in other respects. But we did it. I was still full of anger and self-pity then, and it became harder and harder to go to church and feel anything less than rage. I walked out of the church to sit in the halls and wait for my family on more than one occasion because I didn't know how to process the injustices that I perceived.

Not long after that was the Boy Scout convention. We stopped attending services and slowly withdrew to begin our crash course in the legal process. It was not an easy time, but it was a useful time. It helped me clarify my own perception of who I was and who I was meant to be. I worked through the anger I had held for so many years toward the Church and my parents. I realized that I had been clinging so long to my expectations. The expectation that I was good for nothing. The expectation that God would finally give me a break. These ideas were supposed to be a life preserver, but instead they were dragging me down as surely as if someone had thrown me a manhole cover instead. I learned, in the year that followed, to let them go. When my mind was cleared of this debris, it was easier to separate the members of the church from the church itself. It had been hard for me to sit in church before because I thought of the people in it, the songs, the worship, as part of the same great, monstrous machine. Now I was able to see that love can be practiced by individuals in spite of the religion they subscribe too. I missed the people we met at church and the fellowship and support they willingly offered. I no longer hated the hymns and organ music that had grated on my nerves for so long. In short, I learned, as Les had advised, how to be honest with myself about where the root of my lifelong anguish and suffering really lay.

The thing that still irked me was when anyone tried to describe what God looked like or what God wanted and expected from us. These are the marketing tactics that corporate religion thrusts upon us and we are foolish to tolerate it. When Lola was just two years old and my patience with attending church was at its thinnest, we were all in the car together on our way to a service. These thoughts had been running through my head and I'd always been one to say what's on my mind. I pulled the car over and I turned around to look at my daughters in the backseat.

"Girls, I want you to remember something. Nobody can tell you who God is. They can share their beliefs, but the truth is not one of us knows who God is. And if any of us did it would probably be Lola because she's seen him last."

Lola beamed at me in the back seat, proud as can be. Since then, I made sure that our daughters knew that their relationship with God was theirs and theirs alone. We didn't attended church after that, but we encouraged the girls to go to church with their friends if they wanted to. We always gave them the choice.

The church didn't back off of course, in spite of our non-attendance, but I knew it was not for any deep-seated desire they had to save my soul. Two members from our ward came to the door one day in the midst of our legal pursuit and said, "Tommy, we've come because we have a calling for you."

I was willing to be humored. "Sure, what've you got?"

"Well, we feel that you've been called to an assistant scoutmaster position."

I burst out laughing, but the two young men stared at me blankly.

"Come on," I said, "Who put you up to this?"

They looked at each other and it was clear they were clueless.

"Look, I appreciate it, but no," I said more firmly.

To their credit, they did as they were trained to do. They started to push back, giving me all the reasons why I should just consider an opportunity to give back to the church. I stopped them right there.

"Guys, this is not your fault. I know you're doing what you think you're supposed to do, but I'm not the guy you're looking for. I'm involved in a legal action against the Church. You may have heard?"

They hemmed and hawed. Of course they had heard. Word travels quickly.

"So, I'm sorry you've had to waste your time, but I won't be answering the Church's calling."

"But, God asks—"

"No, he doesn't."

A brief pause. "Is—is there anything we can do?"

It was my turn to consider. "Well, yes, there's a lot that can be done. But I don't know if you two alone could do it."

I dismissed the gentlemen and shut the door. It was an ironic little incident, but aren't they all? I went inside the house, fueled by a new idea. And I sat down to write my story.

EPILOGUE

Arlene and I have been forthright with the girls, especially Sophia, who is a teenager now and capable of understanding the highs and lows we've been through. We tell all four of the girls that we've made enough mistakes for all of them; we started at the bottom and the only place they can go from here is up. They are proving us right. We've made great strides in opening ourselves up and seeing our daughters for the many possibilities they represent for the future, and not for the expectation that they will conform to some image we've conjured up of who they should be.

My life has effectively come full circle in these last years. God works in mysterious but obvious ways. Everything that has come to me has been hard-earned. The healing that began with Les turned into a process of recognition. My sole therapy for the previous two decades had been prayer and the twelve-step program I learned through recovery. Both encouraged a sort of transparency that was born from a desire to understand. I wanted to understand where I'd gone wrong and how I could be better. In doing so, I tried to be aware of my past and clear in the path I took in dealing with it. I talked about my past openly to anyone who would listen, hoping to gain further understanding. But, still, I lacked a foundational knowledge of what it was that was at the very core of my lifelong struggles.

Through Les, and his astounding wisdom, I began to do as he said and come clean with myself. And in doing so, I found the root of my anger. It was at the Boy Scouts of America convention that I realized exactly how deep the damage went. It was then that I was able to see clearly that I was no longer angry with Craig Mathias, but with the institution that allowed him and others like him to perpetuate a legacy of trauma against innocents, when they had every resource available at their disposal to stop it. That was the resoundingly deep, dark truth of the matter. When the realization hit me, I inhaled and felt like I was breathing for the first time.

In the end, I can see that there have been layers of neglect. But there is no blame left to be placed. I have spent many years forgiving Craig Mathias and my parents, and even the Church for the parts they played. I can say that I've achieved forgiveness, but I cannot say that I hold them inculpable. Craig was a sick man and perhaps still is, though he has been punished for his crimes in the eyes of the law and subsequently released to live his life. My parents have endured and suffered with me, but I have peace in knowing that they would have done things differently had they known the course my life would take as a result. Their thoughts and actions were a direct product of the religion they subscribed too.

The Church alone has shown no remorse or inclination to change. Churches, after all, are corporations. They are precluded from caring about people by their sheer preoccupation with membership numbers and the almighty dollar. It's a profitable industry; one that can't seem to practice the compassion that they preach. What's worse, the legal system is set up in such a way that makes it easy for the corporate religions not to care. The money and power and greed that fuels these institutions circulates at such a high level we might as well be grasping at clouds to try and get any recompense.

At the point in our legal battle when I sought Dan Fasy, I had the recognition I wanted by the church, but not the compensation. I still wanted it to hurt them. I wanted them to remember me. But justice doesn't work that way and compassion isn't found in the coffers of the Mormon Church. In contacting Dan Fasy, I did what I had been hesitant to do before. I mailed all of the documentation related to my case to him and left the ball in his court. He agreed to represent me.

At that point, the opposing council were trying to depose the man who had sent Craig Mathias home from his mission so many years ago. He was 98 years old and in failing health. The attorneys petitioned the court to subpoena him and made frantic attempts to secure his testimony. When they finally got ahold of his daughter, she told them that her father had only recently been placed in a care facility and that his memory was questionable at best. He did, however, keep records. From these records, they were able to determine that Craig was sent home because his father requested him to be. That was it. Was I crazy to think that such a cut and dry explanation was still clouded with nuance?

The same anticlimactic legal maneuvering continued, but rather than the battle royale I envisioned, it looked like a tame game of table tennis, the ball being batted back and forth without any real gusto. I still had faith that justice might be served. Once again, my expectations paved the way for my disappointment.

On October 11, 2013, I was due to leave on a business trip to Tucson. I woke early that morning and began the long drive in a loaded, fifty-three foot trailer. I arrived late Friday afternoon and had the evening to relax in the small hotel, before waking early again the next day to begin setting up for the convention. As a labor foreman for a general contractor specializing in the setup of large, professional conventions and conferences, I was responsible for my team of laborers and for securing equipment and additional labor for the setup of these events. Ordinarily I didn't have to travel far for these events, but on this occasion I was not due to dismantle, load, and return to my home in Gilbert until Tuesday evening.

So many things had come to pass in recent months and while the past had never been truly buried, it had at least been relegated to the background where it belonged. And then everything changed...again. There had been, for the previous year, a window open to me. All the years I could have pursued my case I'd spent trying to kill the residual pain. By the time I sobered up, the statute of limitation had expired. Then, Senate Bill 131 in California had been devised in 2012, allowing for an extended statute of limitations on child sexual abuse cases and creating an avenue for many like myself to seek justice for the crimes that had been perpetrated against us as minors and which were largely ignored by the institutions that helped to conceal these crimes when they first occurred. As a result, Arlene and I had a tumultuous year, complete with legal and personal drama, which was now coming to a close as

Senate Bill 131 faced the chopping block. If the bill were vetoed, it would end our year-long struggle to achieve some sort of closure for my own case. I would be effectively barred by the statute of limitation from bringing my case to court.

I had been watching SB-131 like a hawk for the past twelve months. The bill had been presented to the California Senate by Jim Beall of San Jose around March of 2013 and faced powerful opposition from day one. Now Governor Brown had until midnight on Sunday, October 13, 2013, to either veto, sign, or let the bill automatically pass into law. In the quiet hotel room, I was eager for a long awaited opportunity for myself and others like me to be heard.

Friday night, I glued myself to my phone, calling Jerry Brown's office repeatedly to express my views and hopes that he would do the right thing, and checked the California Legislature website for updates in between. After I talked to Arlene that night and told her nothing had been confirmed yet, I got into bed realizing the futility of staying awake for something that may or may not happen. I had to be up early in the morning.

When I did awake, it was with a start. Earlier than usual of course. My body had been so long accustomed to unhealthy hours induced artificially by alcohol and other substances that it no longer seemed to regulate itself according to any set rhythm. Knowing that I would be unable to get back to sleep, I took up my phone again and googled California Legislature. I could tell immediately that something had changed. The site was in the process of updating. It took what felt like forever to do so. I rose and sat on the edge of the bed with my feet on the floor staring at that small glowing screen in an otherwise dark and unfamiliar room. How many times had I clung to such a small and tentative hope?

The screen flashed to life; my hope faltered. During my struggle to achieve normalcy, I had formed a network of people like myself who longed to see justice done, and if not justice, at least recognition, and if not recognition, well...where would we be then? I tossed my phone aside and put my head in my hands. It was too early to feel so shattered. It was at least too early to wake Arlene and tell her the bad news. I was alone, again.

My phone rang and it was Arlene. Of course it was.

"I couldn't sleep," she said, "I already saw that he vetoed it. The coward."

I could hardly speak around the sudden swell of emotion. Arlene had long been my salvation and here she was again, willingly sharing in the rise and fall of our ordinary, extraordinary life. We talked for several more moments, in which I tried to articulate the things I never quite could. And when we hung up, I rose from the bed and pulled open the curtains over the wide window. I could resonate with the darkness, but I also craved life and the sheer audacity of living. Another sunny morning was dawning in Arizona and I could feel the heat on my face. I closed my eyes. Every ending is a new beginning. It happened to me many times, that feeling of stepping into the light. Life, it seems, is full of awakenings.

Governor Brown of California, and those opposed to the passing of SB-131, argued that it was unfair to churches and the other private institutions in which the sexual abuse occurred to open up the statute of limitations. But I can assure you that for the individuals who are affected, the issue was not as easily resolved as it was on paper that Monday morning.

The failure of SB-131 to pass had been the final nail to seal my case shut. I had to face facts. In the end, I choose to see Dan Fasy as a hero, because I have to have a hero in all of this. He is one of the few out there representing me and people like me—the victims who have come to a realization that something must change. Once the hammer came down from the powers that be and SB-131 was reneged, and without an extended statute of limitations, I had little to support my claim. Fasy, the Church and I came to a mutual agreement, and put the case to bed once and for all. I realized the fight could not be won on the basis of dollars and cents. There's so much fluff and drama put on legal matters, but it's all just a show to hide the formulaic process; the agreed upon standards for categorizing and solving disputes. If I'd had the leverage, I would have loved to see Dan Fasy in action, in trial, fighting for the truth. All I would have had to do was show up and look people dead in the eye and face to face with the truth. Instead, my case got put on a shelf with a neat little bow, alongside so many others.

In truth, I can see that money isn't everything. Money does not make us whole. No amount of money from the Church of Jesus Christ of Latter Day Saints could have undone the damage of their negligence and the debilitating effects it had on my life, but it was all they had to offer. Money is a resource. I simply wonder when they will choose to do the right thing with it. I wonder what they are waiting for. I see now that God planned something more for me. He took me in a direction I didn't expect. I would never have chosen to bring this part of my life to the forefront, but it's been up to God, or the universe, or whatever power you believe in. I have found it impossible to ignore the existence of an orchestrator greater than myself to put these events in motion and bring them so seamlessly around so that I can stand here today and see that everything had its purpose, and so have I.

All of this is to say that I strive every day, every moment, to reach the pinnacle, which is being useful. No matter what the results, or how big, our usefulness to others is the only true measure of success. I have been inspired to create change in the world and to see change in myself. There have been many who were instrumental in the process and who will continue to be. I have been transformed by the compassion of my sponsors and moved by speakers I've heard. I've been enlightened by Buddhist and Hindu ideas and teachings, which are refreshingly secular and universal. Meditation has taught me to look within and discover a new source of unlimited power and strength. I have learned that there are people out there who are actually *doing* something. There are people out there like Marci Hamilton, who are fighting for statute of limitations reform, hoping to allow victims of childhood sex abuse to speak when they are ready and to find justice in doing so regardless of how much time has passed.

So often in the midst of our own personal tragedies, we ask ourselves why. I believe I have found my answer. Compassion is a realization I have come to after so many years of self-centered desperation. Now I look at others and see the shame and guilt they carry. I see how affected people are; how damaged by the traumas they've had to face, and I don't understand how we can't all be moved to action.

Through all of this, my parents have continued to say, "Don't forget who did this to you." How could I? We lock the criminals in prison, we talk about what they've done, but is the world really better for it? There are those among us who remain silent, and so much on the subject is left unsaid because we feel that we have locked one more bogeyman away. The media covers these salacious news stories, churches preach intimidation and sell us God like a snake oil remedy, all to take the sting out of how easy we find it to shirk responsibility. All of this just perpetuates the cycle of fear and anger. We must remember that negligence, too, is a punishable crime, but defense attorneys have had their day in court, punishing victims for not coming forward sooner. Lawmakers have upheld the statutes of limitations in cases like mine, forcing people like me back into the silence that has been so deafening and deadening to us for most of our lives. But when the anger and the fear are stripped away, there is nothing left but to see the truth for what it is. We can be our own salvation.

Out beyond ideas of wrongdoing and rightdoing there is a field. I'll meet you there. -Rumi

Downtown Chicago circa 1988

Me and Dad at Sizzler in Hollywood in 2000

Mom and me on Dad's bike during a visit to their house in 2002

Our wedding on June 19, 2004

Rich, Julia and me on a visit to L.A. in 2005.

**Sophia, Lola, Julia, and Fiona
sharing some sister time in 2011.**

Dear Friends of Scouting

We will launch our annual
Friends of Scouting LDS Family
Campaign this coming Sunday.

If you wish to support this worthy cause:

Please come to church prepared to make your
contribution by check, cash or credit card. All
contributions, large and small are welcome.

The need for developing Gospel-centered, patriotic values in
our young men has never been greater. For many years, the
LDS Church has utilized the Scouting Program as the activity
arm of the Aaronic Priesthood to help build boys into worthy,
capable men.

Funds collected in the Friends of Scouting Campaign are
utilized to support the facilities, campsites and activities of the
local Grand Canyon Council, Boy Scouts of America.

*The Church of Jesus Christ of Latter-Day Saints has been
continuously chartered with the Boy Scouts of America since 1913.*

**Boy Scouts fundraising flier found
on our front door**

ACKNOWLEDGMENTS

I want to thank my beautiful wife Arlene, for all her love and support. And also my lovely daughters for supporting me in a thousand sweet and unspoken ways.

I would like to thank Nanda Olney for all her guidance and talent. My publicist, Stacey Champion, has been an inspiration and motivation to finally get this book before the public. Countless people have inspired me along this journey of putting my heart down on the page. Without you this book would not have been written.

My parents deserve my love and devotion and I hope they know they have it always. Family, friends, you know who you are and hopefully I've given you an idea of the balance and fulfillment you bring to my life.

And thank you, the reader. If I have ever met you, you know I love you. If I have not, then I can't wait to!

FOR FURTHER INFORMATION

The following resources have my unmitigated gratitude and remain graciously available for anyone who needs them:

RAINN (24/7)   1-800-656-HOPE (4673)

Empact   (480) 784-1514

National Suicide Prevention Lifeline 1-800-273-8255

For speaking engagements, questions, comments, or assistance, I'll be happy to help:

tomwomjr@gmail.com

scoutsdishonor.com